practices to promote student motiva
accessible textbook should be requi
preparation programs.

tivation

UC President

challenges of motivating their
and compelling book, Eric M.
y and adopt research-based
ts. This wonderful book trans-

A highly practical guide to motivo *to practices that can be imple-*
best research, this excellent book
schools can play a big role in infl
students. Anderman provides a g ᵖᶠessor of Psychology, Stanford University
their students feel efficacious—th Mindset: The New Psychology of Success
of reasonable and even extraoro

—**Carol Dweck**

Regents' Professor Emeritus
Former President of the American Edu
of the National Academ

ι, this book is the perfect mix of
i engaging writing. It asks if you
iem all and considers the core ques-
jroup, to reward, to compete, to fail,
id for teachers, parents, researchers,

—**John Hattie**

or, Melbourne Graduate School of Education
Author, *Visible Learning: A Synthesis of*
800 Meta-Analyses Relating to Achievement

es on teachers' greatest challenge:
nts? Combining more than 30 years
se of classroom realities, he presents
o teachers on how to see motivation
tive and how to influence students'
very teacher who wants to make a
ies of students will find new ways to

—**Thomas Guskey**

Senior Research Scholar, University of Louisville
Professor Emeritus, University of Kentucky
eating Successful Grading and Reporting Systems

vation is an extraordinarily useful sum-
v about academic motivation and how to
the classroom. It is the most comprehen-
k addressing academic motivation on the

—**Jacquelynne S. Eccles**

hed Professor of Education, University of California, Irvine

Sparking
Student Motivation

The Power of Teachers to
Rekindle a Love for Learning

Eric M. Anderman

FOR INFORMATION:

Corwin

A SAGE Company

2455 Teller Road

Thousand Oaks, California 91320

(800) 233-9936

www.corwin.com

SAGE Publications Ltd.

1 Oliver's Yard

55 City Road

London EC1Y 1SP

United Kingdom

SAGE Publications India Pvt. Ltd.

B 1/I 1 Mohan Cooperative Industrial Area

Mathura Road, New Delhi 110 044

India

SAGE Publications Asia-Pacific Pte. Ltd.

18 Cross Street #10-10/11/12

China Square Central

Singapore 048423

Printed in the United States of America

Library of Congress Cataloging-in-Publication Data

Names: Anderman, Eric M., author.

Title: Sparking student motivation : the power of teachers to rekindle alove for learning / Eric M. Anderman.

Description: First edition. | Thousand Oaks, California : Corwin Press, Inc., [2021] | Includes bibliographical references and index.

Identifiers: LCCN 2020025105 | ISBN 9781071803189 (paperback) | ISBN 9781071803233 (epub) | ISBN 9781071803219 (epub) | ISBN 9781071803202 (ebook)

Subjects: LCSH: Motivation in education. | Teacher-student relationships.

Classification: LCC LB1065 .A57 2021 | DDC 370.15/4–dc23

LC record available at https://lccn.loc.gov/2020025105

This book is printed on acid-free paper.

Acquisitions Editor: Eliza B. Erickson

Project Editor: Amy Schroller

Copy Editor: Lynne Curry

Typesetter: Hurix Digital

Proofreader: Dennis Webb

Indexer: Integra

Cover Designer: Candice Harman

Marketing Manager: Sharon Pendergast

20 21 22 23 24 10 9 8 7 6 5 4 3 2 1

CONTENTS

ACKNOWLEDGMENTS

I owe gratitude to numerous individuals who supported my work on this book. First, I am grateful to the numerous colleagues who provided me with invaluable feedback along the way: Kaia Christofferson, Jack Conrath, Melissa Conrath, Naima Khandaker, Steve Kucinski, John Marschhausen, Mary Rykowski, Jennie Tober, Mickie Sebenoler, Kelli Weaver, and Joshua Zollinger. I also am grateful to Eliza Erickson and Ariel Curry at Corwin for believing in this project and providing me with the opportunity to write this book. This work was inspired by my "motivation" mentors whose scholarship continues to inspire me all these years later: Jacquelynne Eccles, Martin Maehr, Carol Midgley, and Paul Pintrich. I am extremely grateful to the countless graduate students who have worked with me on motivation research over the years—I have learned more from you than you will ever realize. I also am grateful to teachers—those who taught me and those whom I continue to have the honor and privilege of working with today. Finally, I am extraordinarily grateful to my two young adults, Jacob and Sarah (since I can't really call you children anymore), and to my partner in everything, Lynley—you all are the greatest joys of my life and you inspire and motivate me every day.

Publisher's Acknowledgments

Corwin gratefully acknowledges the contributions of the following peer reviewers:

Matthew Banach
Principal
Northwest School

Heath Peine
Executive Director of Student Support Services
Wichita Public Schools

Joe Schmidt
Social Studies Specialist
Maine Department of Education

James A. Tucker
McKee Chair of Excellence in Learning, Professor of Educational Psychology
University of Tennessee at Chattanooga

ABOUT THE AUTHOR

 **Eric M. Anderman** is Professor of Educational Psychology and of Quantitative Methods, Evaluation, and Research in the College of Education and Human Ecology at The Ohio State University. He received his PhD in Educational Psychology from The University of Michigan, and he also holds a master's degree from Harvard University and a bachelor of science degree from Tufts University. His research over the past 25 years has focused on academic motivation. He is a fellow of both the American Psychological Association and the American Educational Research Association. He is the editor of the journal *Theory into Practice*, and he recently co-edited the third edition of the *Handbook of Educational Psychology* with Lyn Corno, and the *Visible Learning Guide to Student Achievement* with John Hattie. He is the co-author of three textbooks, as well as more than 100 peer-reviewed articles and invited chapters. His research has been featured in numerous media outlets, including CBS News, NBC News (*Dateline NBC*), CNN, NPR, *The Huffington Post*, *The Wall Street Journal*, *New York* magazine, and numerous other outlets. His research has been funded by a variety of agencies, including the Institute of Education Sciences, the U.S. Department of Health and Human Services, and the National Institutes of Health.

INTRODUCTION

- Jill is 15 years old, and she loves to compose songs on her guitar; playing the guitar is her passion, and she'd rather be strumming on her guitar than doing just about anything else.

- Mateo is 6 years old; his classroom teacher describes Mateo as being bored whenever the class is working on reading lessons in their small groups.

- Sophia is 11 years old; she is very confident and eager to participate when she is playing soccer, but she is the complete opposite when she is working on math homework: she doesn't believe she is good at doing math, and she looks for any excuse that she can to avoid doing math.

- Lucas is 17 years old; he works very hard in his Spanish class, and when he doesn't do well, he generally believes that he should have studied more, and he refocuses his efforts to work even harder.

Do any of these scenarios sound familiar to you? Have you ever encountered a student who often is bored? Or a student who is highly eager to participate in whatever you have planned? Or a student who lacks confidence? As you have probably surmised from the title of this book, all of these scenarios represent different examples of student *motivation*. Jill seems to be highly motivated to compose songs on her guitar, whereas Sophia seems to be anything but motivated to work on math problems; Lucas is clearly motivated to do well in his Spanish class, whereas Mateo is not motivated to read in small groups.

If you were teaching these students, how would you feel about having Jill in your music class? How would you feel about having Sophia in your math class? And how would you feel about having Mateo in your classroom if you were responsible for teaching reading? For many teachers, it is a joy to have a student like Jill in one's class; but for many, dealing with students like Mateo or Sophia might lead to some anxiety.

You don't have to feel embarrassed if you feel a bit reluctant to work with students who do not seem to be motivated. Both students and teachers regularly report that students often are not motivated and that this lack of motivation has a detrimental effect on achievement and class climate (Collier, 2015). In fact, many teachers leave the profession after only a few years in the classroom (Carver-Thomas & Darling-Hammond, 2017), and some of this attrition occurs because teachers become frustrated with how difficult it is to motivate their students.

> This book is about how *you*, as a classroom teacher, can generate a spark of enthusiasm, confidence, and joy in your students.

This book is about students like Sophia and Mateo and Lucas, and many others. But it is also about teachers. This book is about how *you*, as a classroom teacher, can generate a spark of enthusiasm in Mateo; how you can help Sophia to gain confidence in math; and how you can tap into Jill's enthusiasm so that it becomes contagious to your other students.

The Power of a Teacher to Impact Student Motivation

Stop for a moment and think about a teacher that you had (at any point in your life) who influenced your motivation (for better or worse, but hopefully for the better). I ask that question quite often, and I have never met anyone who can't give me a rapid and powerful response. We have all had teachers who have done so much to motivate us.

I'd like to disclose a personal example of a small act of a teacher that made a difference in my life. When I was in high school, I generally did well in my math classes, and I was enrolled in advanced math courses. Once during the tenth grade, I got a lower than usual grade on a major test in my math class; now this wasn't a terrible or failing grade, but I certainly scored lower than I usually did. To my utter surprise, my math teacher came over to me, and quietly said, "What happened Eric? This isn't like you; I know you can do better. I was really surprised by your grade on this test." Whereas some students might cringe at a comment like this, it was just what I needed to hear, and my math teacher knew that. This teacher knew that I had probably just goofed off and not studied as much as I should have (and she was probably correct). Her brief comments had an impact on me and energized me to work harder and to achieve an "A" grade for the year in math.

But as I reflect on this, I often wonder why I still remember this so vividly and why I was so surprised that she took the time to notice my less than stellar performance on one exam (after all, I didn't fail the test; I just didn't quite perform as well as I usually did.) What I have come to realize is that I still remember this because this teacher took time to notice and to care—*and to tell me that she noticed and she cared.* She also knew me as an individual—she knew that these small comments would be all I needed to get back on track. I'm still grateful today for this caring teacher; she knew something important about motivation, and she knew what to do to get me going again. Of course, not all situations are as simple and straightforward as the one that I just described. Many students need more than just a brief comment from the teacher to motivate them.

Rationale for This Book

I have spent the past three decades conducting research on student motivation. My "study" of motivation began when I worked as a classroom teacher; it then continued when I went to graduate school and spent five years studying and researching this topic. This has continued for the past 25 years; I have devoted my academic research career to the study of academic motivation. Moreover, as a parent, I have observed firsthand how my own children have displayed varying degrees of motivation for different subject areas over the years.

One theme has consistently emerged for me across all of these experiences: *Teachers affect student motivation!* We can make a difference in our students' lives and help them to achieve and exceed their goals. There is an extraordinarily consistent body of research that examines academic motivation; the goal of this book is to translate that research into practical strategies, so that you can be one of those teachers who makes a difference.

> We can make a difference in our students' lives and help them to achieve and exceed their goals.

Motivation quiz. Let's stop for a moment and take a brief quiz about motivation. See if you can answer the questions presented in Figure 0.1.

The answers to the quiz are presented at the end of the chapter (you can look ahead now and check yourself). Were you surprised by some of the correct answers? Were you surprised by how many times "IT DEPENDS" was the right answer? As you will see throughout this book, motivation often does "depend" on the individual student and the specific situation. Whereas my math teacher's brief comments to me were enough to motivate me to do better on my next math exam, another student in the same class might need something quite different.

Everything that is included in this book is based on sound, peer-reviewed, empirical research, but is presented in a way that is incredibly practical and approachable. You will not find an abundance of research jargon, theoretical musings, or citations beyond what is necessary to undergird the strategies presented in each chapter. Throughout the book, you will find Motivation Myth sections that dispel many of the unsubstantiated beliefs

Figure 0.1 Motivation Quiz

1. When teachers reward their students for completing an assignment, students will be motivated to complete another similar assignment.	TRUE	FALSE	IT DEPENDS
2. If a student has reached high school and is thoroughly convinced that she/he can't learn a foreign language, there isn't much hope of changing that student's mind.	TRUE	FALSE	IT DEPENDS
3. If a student doesn't like a specific subject area (e.g., chemistry), the student won't be motivated in that class.	TRUE	FALSE	IT DEPENDS
4. A student can both enjoy doing a task and be motivated to get a good grade on the task.	TRUE	FALSE	IT DEPENDS
5. Motivation changes as children move from elementary school into middle school and high school.	TRUE	FALSE	IT DEPENDS
6. Whenever you test students on content, you are harming their motivation to learn that content.	TRUE	FALSE	IT DEPENDS
7. Student motivation is influenced by the people with whom a student interacts while working on a task.	TRUE	FALSE	IT DEPENDS
8. If a student is highly interested in a particular subject area (e.g., science), the student is likely to learn a lot and get good grades in that subject area.	TRUE	FALSE	IT DEPENDS
9. Students are motivated by competition.	TRUE	FALSE	IT DEPENDS
10. Students will learn more and be more motivated to continue studying about a topic if we match our instructional methods with the students' preferred learning styles.	TRUE	FALSE	IT DEPENDS

that exist about student motivation (some of them are alluded to in the quiz that you just took!).

Organization of the Book

This book is organized into two parts. The first part of the book serves as an introduction to motivation, while the second part of the book focuses on strategies that teachers can use in their classrooms on a daily basis.

Part I is divided into four chapters. In the first chapter, I define and explain motivation. Specifically, after examining some textbook definitions of "motivation," we will examine some of the underlying processes that contribute to and direct academic motivation in our students. Readers are asked, both in this chapter and throughout the book, to think about their own personal motivation, along with their students' motivation. *A major theme throughout this book is that in order for teachers to effectively motivate students, they need to understand the sources of their own motivation.* Each chapter contains activities and exercises that will encourage you to reflect on both your students' motivation as well as your own motivation (across different contexts of your life).

> In order for teachers to be able to effectively motivate students, teachers need to understand the sources of their own motivation.

In the second chapter, I examine a question that is often forgotten: "Who shapes student motivation?" It is often assumed that students come to school either highly motivated to learn or not motivated to learn. In this chapter, I examine the influences of teachers and parents on student academic motivation. In Chapter 3, we will explore the role of students' beliefs about their own abilities, and how those beliefs affect their motivation to learn. This chapter builds upon Chapter 2 where I discuss the roles that we, as teachers, play in shaping these beliefs. Chapter 4 focuses on the content that we teach and how students feel about that. Most of the time we are bound by curriculum, and that curriculum is limited to the subject area and grade level that we are currently teaching. Nevertheless, there is still a great deal that you can do to make the curriculum interesting and engaging for your students. One of the important ideas that I discuss in this chapter is the notion of *utility value*; although we, as teachers, understand why we are teaching specific content, students often do not see the relevance of what we are teaching. As I discuss in this chapter, there are several simple strategies that you can employ to help your students understand the value of what they are learning; when students value what you are teaching, their motivation will improve.

In the second part of the book, you will learn how to put this information into practice. Each of the remaining chapters focuses specifically on the roles of the classroom teacher in supporting student motivation. The chapters are written so that teachers can use this information to inform daily classroom practice. Part II will provide you with strategies to use with your students and prompt you to think about your own experiences in school when you were a student and your own motivation; this will help you to more effectively apply the strategies that are introduced in each chapter to your daily routines.

Chapter 5 ("How Should I Teach?") focuses on the ways that we present content to our students. In this chapter, I examine routine practices such as group work and the use of rewards and competition. I specifically look at the ways in which these practices affect student motivation. In this chapter, you will encounter some suggestions that may encourage you to make some minor changes to some of your current practices (e.g., how you incorporate technology into instruction); these minor changes can lead to remarkably positive shifts in student motivation.

At this point, you are probably already saying to yourself that this all *sounds* great, but *as a teacher, I have to give tests, and students sometimes are not motivated to take tests.* This is where Chapter 6 comes into play ("What About Testing?"). In this chapter, I confront the apparent conflict between motivation and testing. You'll be asked to reflect on some of your own experiences with test-taking in this chapter (hopefully this won't bring back too many painful memories!). I then discuss the purposes of testing and some of the reasons why various forms of assessment have a negative impact on student motivation. And I confront the often dreaded topic of standardized tests and high-stakes assessments. I'll also provide you with many research-based strategies that will help you to make assessments a pleasant experience for your students.

In Chapter 7 ("Should I Be Nice?") I examine teacher-student relationships. Teachers often wonder about the types of relationships that they should have with their students (How friendly should I be? Should I smile before the holidays? Should I ask students on Monday how their weekend went?). These questions are significant; the types of relationships that we have with our students do matter. We'll examine this in some depth and discuss the ways in which your relationships with your students affect their academic motivation.

In Chapter 8 ("What About Behavior Management?"), I discuss the relations between student behavior and academic motivation. Although as teachers we often think about behavior management and academic motivation as separate concepts, they are intricately tied to each other. In this chapter, we'll talk about the reciprocal relationships between student behavior and motivation. You'll also learn several strategies that may help you to rethink some classroom rules and procedures. By the end of the chapter, you'll see that it is possible to have an orderly classroom and also to have students who want to learn and participate in your lesson.

The final chapter ("How Do I Make This All Work?") will help you to think about how you can tie all of this information together, and strategically approach your daily lesson planning so that you can foster positive motivation in your students. In this chapter, I discuss how to balance the needs of individual students with the needs of the entire class.

Some Final Words

Students' motivational beliefs emerge when children enter preschool, and they continue to develop over time (Stipek, 2011; Wigfield & Eccles, 2002). As a classroom teacher, you have great power in shaping students' motivation. Whereas some children come to believe from an early age that they are not good at schoolwork (or perhaps that they are not good at learning a particular subject like reading), as a classroom teacher you have the ability to change this.

> As a classroom teacher, you have great power in shaping students' motivation.

Whether you teach very young children who are first forming motivational beliefs, older children who are exploring their interests and abilities, or adolescents who have developed strong beliefs about what they can and can't do, you can make a difference! This book focuses on all of these students, and the many strategies that you can employ to positively impact your students' lives.

Figure 0.2 Motivation Quiz With Answers

The correct answer to each question is bolded. We will return to this quiz in Chapter 9 to re-examine your responses and how your thinking may have changed.			
1. When teachers reward their students for completing an assignment, students will be even more motivated to complete another similar assignment.	TRUE	FALSE	IT DEPENDS
2. If a student has reached high school and is thoroughly convinced that she/he can't learn a foreign language, there isn't much hope of changing that student's mind.	TRUE	FALSE	IT DEPENDS

(Continued)

Figure 0.2 (Continued)

3. If a student doesn't like a specific subject area (e.g., chemistry), the student won't be motivated in that class.	TRUE	FALSE	IT DEPENDS
4. A student can both enjoy doing a task and be motivated to get a good grade on the task.	TRUE	FALSE	IT DEPENDS
5. Motivation changes as children move from elementary school into middle school and high school.	TRUE	FALSE	IT DEPENDS
6. Whenever you test students on content, you are harming their motivation to learn that content.	TRUE	FALSE	IT DEPENDS
7. Student motivation is influenced by the people with whom a student interacts while working on a task.	TRUE	FALSE	IT DEPENDS
8. If a student is highly interested in a particular subject area (e.g., science), the student is likely to learn a lot and get good grades in that subject area.	TRUE	FALSE	IT DEPENDS
9. Students are motivated by competition.	TRUE	FALSE	IT DEPENDS
10. Students will learn more and be more motivated to continue studying about a topic if we match our instructional methods with the students' preferred learning styles.	TRUE	FALSE	IT DEPENDS

PART I
AN INTRODUCTION TO MOTIVATION

WHAT IS MOTIVATION? CHAPTER 1

Have you ever met a teacher who did not care about student motivation? Probably not. Student motivation is something that every teacher thinks about. We all want our students to look forward to coming to our classes, to be engaged and participate during our lessons, and to want to come back again and learn more tomorrow. But is that what you experience on a daily basis? Do your students all seem overjoyed to be in your classroom and to engage in whatever lesson you have prepared for them? Or do they sometimes stare longingly at the clock and look like they'd rather be at recess?

In this chapter, we will begin our exploration of student motivation—both what it is, and what it isn't. We'll do this by first examining your own motivation. Next, we will begin to deconstruct the concept of "motivation," so that you can begin to see that your students' motivation involves a number of beliefs and behaviors. Third, we will discuss some other processes that are similar to but not exactly the same as motivation. While you may feel that you already are familiar with some of the topics that you're about to read about, it's important for you to reassess your familiarity with some seemingly basic concepts about motivation and to think about them both in terms of your own personal motivation, and your students' motivation.

Understanding Your Own Motivation

A theme that you will repeatedly encounter throughout this book is that teachers can most effectively support positive motivation in their students if they first understand their own personal motivation. In other words, if you understand why you personally are motivated across a variety of situations, you'll be better able to both understand and support your students. Let's start our exploration of motivation by doing the following exercise; there are no right or wrong answers:

Activity 1.1 Motivation Items

Based on your current understanding of motivation, on a scale of 1 (unmotivated) to 5 (highly motivated), how motivated would you be to do each of the following?

	Unmotivated	Slightly Motivated	Somewhat Motivated	Very Motivated	Extremely Motivated
Read that book that has been on your "summer reading list" for the last few summers.	1	2	3	4	5
Enroll in a challenging graduate-level course on organic chemistry.	1	2	3	4	5
Swim with sharks.	1	2	3	4	5
Learn how to meditate.	1	2	3	4	5
Take a trip to Moscow.	1	2	3	4	5

Now look over your responses. You might have put 5s down for some of these items that you'd really love to do, and 1s for some others that you might never want to attempt; and you probably put responses in the range of 2 through 4 for activities that you might consider doing.

Although these items were probably easy for you to think about, some other people who responded to the same items might have responded very differently than you did. Let's take a look at some differing responses to these items.

In looking at these responses, please note that we are looking at extremes—those people who responded with a "1" (very low motivation for the activity) and with a "5" (very high motivation for the activity). Many respondents (including you) probably responded to some of the items with 2s, 3s, or 4s; but let's go with the extremes for now so that we can look closely at variations in motivation. When you read through the descriptions of the respondents' reasons for answering either "1" or "5," what

Activity 1.1 (Continued) Sample Responses to Motivation Items

Item	Responded "1" (Low Motivation)	Responded "5" (High Motivation)
Read that book that has been on your "summer reading list" for the last few summers.	Elijah knows he probably should read the book, but he really thought about it, and even though all of his friends read it, he finally admitted to himself that he really doesn't think it sounds very interesting.	Ozzie keeps hearing from his friends that this is a life-changing book; the topic is interesting to him, so he finally decides to just pick it up and read it.
Enroll in a challenging graduate-level course on organic chemistry.	Andrew is terrified about taking a difficult science course; he never felt that he was very good at learning science, and he has absolutely no desire to work hard for a course on organic chemistry that he feels he will fail anyway.	Tracey is fascinated by the human body; she wants to learn all that she can about the chemistry that supports our life functions.
Swim with sharks.	George is shocked that this is even a remote possibility; he is afraid of sharks and couldn't imagine doing this.	Donna is a thrill-seeker; this sounds very exciting to her, and she would love to do this.
Learn how to meditate.	Harper thinks meditating is a huge waste of time; he feels that even one brief attempt at meditating would be dreadfully boring.	Keira has always wanted to learn how to meditate; her favorite cousin has been meditating for years and never misses a day. Keira admires her cousin's passion for life and feels that meditation may improve her own outlook on life as well.
Take a trip to Moscow.	Kaylee is not at all eager to travel to Moscow; she has no confidence in her ability to apply for both a passport and a visa, to go through customs in Russia, and to even find her way out of the airport in a foreign country.	Yujin loves to travel and to explore new places; she would buy her tickets and leave for Moscow tomorrow if she could.

stands out to you? Are all of these people motivated in the same way? Clearly, they are not!

Now let's do the next part of this exercise. In each of the boxes in the table above, write down one or two words (under each description) that describe *the reasons* for each person's very low motivation (the 1s) or very high motivation (the 5s). So, for example, for the first item, what one or two words describe why Elijah ultimately decided not to read the book? What one or two words describe why Ozzie decided to finally read the book?

Now, look over the words that you wrote in the 10 boxes. The first thing that most people notice is that the words are not the same! These 10 people all had very different reasons for either wanting to (or not wanting to) engage in these activities. Some of the words or phrases that you may have come up with may resemble the following:

Table 1.1 Possible Reasons for Responses to Motivation Items

Item	Responded "1"	Responded "5"
Read that book that has been on your "summer reading list" for the last few summers.	Elijah • Not interested • Not worth the time • Better things to do	Ozzie • Interested • Feels inspired by friends
Enroll in a challenging graduate-level course on organic chemistry.	Andrew • Anxiety • Fear of failure • Lack of confidence • Nobody he knows would do this	Tracey • Wants to get a good grade • Eager to learn • Confident
Swim with sharks.	George • Fear • Anxiety	Donna • Excited • Will be fun
Learn how to meditate.	Harper • Boring • Not worth the time	Keira • Inspired • Goal-oriented
Take a trip to Moscow.	Kaylee • Fear • Lack of confidence	Yujin • Fun • Because friends went and loved it • Confident

It is probably becoming clear to you now that *people are motivated in many different ways, and for many different reasons.* Sometimes we may be motivated to do something because it is interesting or might be fun; sometimes we're motivated to do something because it represents a goal that we have (something on our bucket list); and sometimes we're motivated to do things because we are confident that we will be successful. In contrast, in some situations we may be motivated *not* to do things because we might lack confidence, be uninterested in the activity or topic, be afraid, or be reluctant because we see no relevance in the activity. There are many other reasons (beyond the ones that you came up with or that are mentioned above) as to why people might decide to engage in the activities presented in this exercise.

Just as you are motivated differently across situations, so are your students. Motivation isn't simply whether or not a student wants to (or does not want to) engage in certain activities at school; as you will see throughout this book, motivation involves our needs, our beliefs, our goals, and our behaviors. In addition, motivation is influenced by our surroundings, our cultures, and our relationships and interactions with others; for example, Keira was motivated to learn how to meditate *because of the influence of her cousin*—if Keira did not have a relationship with her meditation-loving cousin, then she might never have decided to give meditation a try!

Defining Motivation

There are many textbook definitions of motivation. Here are a few examples:

- *"Motivation is the process whereby goal-directed activities are instigated and sustained"* (Schunk, Meece, & Pintrich, 2014, p. 5).

- *"Motivation is a theoretical construct used to explain the initiation, direction, intensity, persistence, and quality of behavior, especially goal-directed behavior"* (Maehr & Meyer, 1997, as cited in Brophy, 2004, p. 3).

- *"Motivation is a theogretical concept that accounts for why people (or animals) choose to engage in particular behaviors at particular times"* (Beck, 2000, p. 3).

These and other similar definitions of motivation are scientifically accurate and undergird the research that supports all of the strategies that will be discussed in this book. Nevertheless, definitions of this nature are theoretical and do not immediately bring to mind applications for classroom practice. Moreover, although most of us (both educators and non-educators) have a general understanding of human motivation, much of what the general public believes about motivation is actually somewhat inaccurate (Pink, 2009).

So, let's take a different approach as we begin our exploration of motivation. Instead of focusing on a broad, conceptual definition of "motivation," let's deconstruct the idea and look at some of the core components that contribute to motivation.

Needs

We all have many needs. Let's take a moment to think about what you might need in various contexts. Think about how you would answer these three questions:

1. What do you *need* to successfully complete your work for today? (whatever work that might be—work for your job, work at home, etc.)
2. What do you *need* in order to survive for one month?
3. What do you *need* in order to be happy?

Jot down your answers to each of these questions, and then look carefully at your answers; do any themes emerge?

Let's take a look at some typical answers to these questions (see Table 1.2).

Do your responses resemble the examples in Table 1.2? There is probably some overlap. What should be clear is that we have many needs, and those needs vary, depending on the context. Obviously, all humans need supplies like food and water and shelter for survival; but those of us with jobs also have needs in order to get our jobs done (e.g., time to complete our work!). And most of us want to be happy... but different people have different needs for happiness. For some people, friends might

Table 1.2 Examples of Needs

1. What do you need to successfully complete your work for today?	• Time to complete tasks • Few distractions • Laptop • Cooperation from coworkers
2. What do you need in order to survive for one month?	• Food • Water • Shelter • Air
3. What do you need in order to be happy?	• Family • Friends • Downtime

be a great source of happiness; for others, relaxation time might be important.

Motivation researchers have identified needs as core components of human motivation. We are all motivated to meet our needs. Let's look more closely at the responses for question #2 (*What do you need in order to survive for one month?*). Given the importance of food and water for survival, humans are certainly motivated to meet those needs; if someone does not have any food, that person will surely be motivated to find food. But we are also motivated to find ways to meet our other needs. Let's look at the responses to question #1 (*What do you need in order to successfully complete your work today?*). If you are a diligent worker, you will want to get your job completed; therefore, if your office environment is noisy, you'd be motivated to find a quiet place to work (to fulfill your "need" for few distractions); if you need others to partner with you to complete a task, you'll be motivated to gain cooperation from your coworkers.

MASLOW'S HIERARCHY OF NEEDS

One of the most well-known needs-based frameworks for understanding motivation is Maslow's hierarchy of needs (see Figure 1.1).

The needs at the bottom of the figure (e.g., physiological needs) represent our most basic needs (e.g., the need for food, water, etc.). We are motivated by these needs, and the needs diminish in priority as one moves up the hierarchy. Physiological needs are the most important for survival, followed by the need for safety, the need to feel loved and experience a sense of belonging, the need for esteem (i.e., the need to feel good about yourself and for others also to believe that other people see you in a positive light), and finally the need for self-actualization (i.e., to be all that you can be; to fulfill your destiny) (Maslow, 1954). According to Maslow, we will only be motivated to satisfy the

Figure 1.1 Maslow's Hierarchy of Needs

needs at the top of the hierarchy once the more basic needs at the lower levels have been met.

Maslow's hierarchy is a useful rubric to think about how we are motivated by our needs (and for how your students are motivated by their needs). The hierarchy makes sense, in that most of us will be motivated to meet the needs for food, safety, and love, before we'd be motivated to meet a self-actualization need (e.g., becoming a poet). Nevertheless, it is important to recognize that Maslow's hierarchy was not developed based on empirical research. The hierarchy was developed through a theoretical lens and is based more on Maslow's opinions than on empirical research. Although the hierarchy isn't very scientific and is not referenced much in contemporary research on academic motivation, it serves as a useful reminder of the importance of needs when trying to understand student motivation.

Let's look at an example of how the hierarchy might be useful. Teachers often encounter students whose families do not have sufficient resources and may be living in poverty. These students may come to school hungry; your students are not going to be highly motivated to engage in the lesson that you have planned for them if all that they can think about is how hungry they are. As we move through the book, it will be important for you to remember that if your students' basic needs (e.g., physiological needs and the need for safety) are not met, it is going to be difficult for them to be motivated to concentrate on the lesson that you prepared for that day.

 STRATEGY 1.1

Basic Needs

Are your students coming to school ready to learn? Can you talk to your students about their lives at home? It is often difficult to know if and how a classroom teacher should have conversations with students about personal information (e.g., whether a student has had breakfast). You need to understand the parameters within your own school and school district about what is and is not appropriate. Talk to a school social worker, school psychologist, or an administrator about these parameters, particularly if you suspect that a student's basic needs may not be met at home. Working together with others, you can assess these situations, and arrange for possible services (e.g., free breakfast at school) to support these students so that they can be optimally motivated to learn in your class. We'll go into greater depth about how to have these conversations in Chapter 7.

Maslow's hierarchy is one way to think about how our needs affect our motivation; however, there are other frameworks that are somewhat more useful in discussions of students' academic motivation. One of the most useful frameworks is *self-determination theory* (Ryan & Deci, 2017). We'll take a deeper dive into this theory and strategies that you can use to motivate your students later in this book. Right now, I want to point out to you that this theory (and a tremendous amount of research that supports the theory) is framed around three needs that are tied to academic motivation:

1. The need for autonomy. Students are more optimally motivated when they can make choices and be involved in decision-making; their motivation suffers when they feel as though they are always being monitored and controlled by teachers.

2. The need for competence. Students are more optimally motivated when they feel that they are succeeding in their academic work; in other words, when students truly see that they are learning (i.e., becoming competent), their motivation improves.

3. The need for relatedness. Students are more optimally motivated when they feel connected to others; in other words, students want to feel like they belong in your classroom and at school.

We'll come back to these three needs later on in the book. But for now, you have learned the first important lesson about human motivation: We have many needs in our lives, and we are motivated, to varying degrees, to fulfill these needs. "Needs" represent one very important aspect of human motivation. Your students have many needs, and as a teacher, you can help fulfill some of those needs.

Beliefs

Although we seldom think about it, our beliefs have a huge impact on our motivation. These include our beliefs about our abilities, our beliefs about whether or not it's worth spending the time doing something, and our beliefs about how the world works. As you'll see throughout the book, your students' beliefs are among the most important determinants of their motivation. Activity 1.2 provides examples of some students' beliefs; read each belief, and then write down an example of how that belief might affect the student's motivation.

> By understanding that your students' beliefs are powerful motivators, you will be able to support their learning by influencing those beliefs.

Activity 1.2 Students' Beliefs

Consider how these students' beliefs might affect their motivation. Write down at least one potential effect of the belief on the student's subsequent motivation.

Student	Belief	Motivational Outcome
Jeffrey, fourth grade	Jeffrey believes that he is not good at sports.	
Marta, ninth grade	Marta believes that it's a waste of time for her to learn math, because she'll never use it in a job.	
Alex, tenth grade	Alex believes that he is dumb and just can't learn.	
Ashley, third grade	Ashley believes that she is a good reader.	
Rebekah, eleventh grade	Rebekah believes that if she works really hard and gets As in all her subjects, she'll go to an Ivy League college and earn over $1 million by the time she is 25.	

These students' beliefs vary in many ways; Alex's belief that he is "dumb" reflects a belief about his ability; Rebekah's belief about getting As reflects her belief that her efforts will result in financial success; Marta's belief that math will not be useful reflects a belief about the value of a school subject. Some potential effects of these beliefs on these students' motivation are presented below:

Activity 1.2 (Continued) Effects of Beliefs on Student Motivation

Student	Belief	Motivational Outcome
Jeffrey, fourth grade	Jeffrey believes that he is not good at sports.	Jeffrey is reluctant to play soccer or baseball.
Marta, ninth grade	Marta believes that it's a waste of time for her to learn math, because she'll never use it in a job.	Marta doesn't study for math tests.
Alex, tenth grade	Alex believes that he is dumb and just can't learn.	Alex drops out of school.

Ashley, third grade	Ashley believes that she is a good reader.	Ashley reads as much as she can at home, even during vacations.
Rebekah, eleventh grade	Rebekah believes that if she works really hard and gets As in all her subjects, she'll go to an Ivy League college and earn over $1 million by the time she is 25.	Rebekah studies diligently every night to keep up her A average.

Students hold many beliefs that affect their motivation. These include beliefs about their abilities, their teachers, their families, their school subjects, and their future plans, just to name a few. You have probably heard about mindsets—that is, students' beliefs about whether or not they can learn just about anything versus the belief that learning is "fixed," such that some students just can't learn as much as others (Dweck, 2016). Mindsets are also beliefs, and they will be discussed in depth in Chapter 5. All of these beliefs are important; as you can see from the examples of effects on motivation in Activity 1.2, these beliefs truly can influence students' behaviors. Sometimes beliefs have a positive effect (e.g., Ashley's belief that she is a good reader leads her to read more and more books); but sometimes beliefs have negative effects (e.g., Alex's prevailing belief that he is "dumb" leads him to eventually drop out of school).

 ## STRATEGY 1.2
Students' Beliefs

Do you really know what your students believe about their ability to learn? You might be surprised to find out that some of your seemingly confident students are actually not as confident as you might think; you also might be surprised to find out that some of your students who do not do well in your class may actually be overly confident about their abilities. Ask your students how much they agree with the following statements three times: before you start a new unit, during the unit, and after completion of the unit. For example, imagine that you are a fourth grade teacher about to begin a unit on the solar system:

1. I am confident that I can learn and understand the unit on the solar system.

   (1 = strongly disagree, 2 = disagree, 3 = unsure, 4 = agree, 5 = strongly agree).

(Continued)

(Continued)

2. Learning about the solar system will be easy for me.

(1 = strongly disagree, 2 = disagree, 3 = unsure, 4 = agree, 5 = strongly agree).

Then, once again ask your students how much they agree with the statements at the middle of the unit, but change the wording to *"I am confident that I am learning and understanding the unit on the solar system,"* and *"Learning about the solar system is easy for me"*; at the end of the unit (or soon after completion of the unit), present the statements a final time, but use the following wording: *"I am confident that I learned and understood the unit on the solar system,"* and *"Learning about the solar system was easy for me."*

It will be very informative for you to look at your students' responses immediately after you ask each set of questions and also to look at how their responses changed over the course of the unit. Are you surprised by any of the students' responses?

P.S.: if you teach young children, (e.g., second grade or younger), sometimes students find it easier to express how much they agree with the statements using a series of smiley-faces rather than with a scale of 1 through 5:

You have now learned another important initial lesson about student motivation: *Students' beliefs matter!* Students' beliefs about many aspects of learning affect their motivation and their achievement; this is true for kindergartners, for middle school students, and for high school seniors. So, you now might be thinking (as many teachers do), *"Oh great, so if motivation is influenced by the beliefs that reside in my students' heads, what can I do about that?"* As you will learn throughout this book, you can do a lot to affect those beliefs. By understanding that your students' beliefs are powerful motivators, you will be able to support their learning by influencing those beliefs.

Goals

The word "goal" is frequently used by most of us, probably several times per week. But what is a goal, and what roles do goals play in understanding our students' motivation? Goals have been defined as "internal representations of desired states" (Austin & Vancouver, 1996, p. 338). Essentially, our goals are our thoughts about what we hope to do or accomplish.

We all have goals. Some of our goals reflect things that we want to accomplish in the short-term; for example, a goal that I have is to mow my lawn this weekend. But some of our goals are longer term in nature; for example, another goal that I have is someday to travel to Greece. And some of our goals are ongoing; for example, I have a goal of eating healthy food and exercising. This is not a goal that I have just for the short-term; it is something that I want to do now, and I want to keep doing in the future.

Therefore, our goals have a temporal element to them. We can have short-term goals (e.g., to mow the lawn this weekend), distant goals (e.g., to someday travel to Greece), and ongoing goals (e.g., to eat healthy food and exercise). All of our goals have the potential to motivate us to engage in behaviors that can help us to realize our goals. Whether or not we act on those goals and engage in the behaviors that are necessary in order to realize our goals depends on a number of variables; we will discuss those variables in depth later in this book.

Our students also have goals, and those goals have the potential to motivate them. Let's take a look at three academic goals that our students might hold (see Table 1.3):

Table 1.3 Examples of Goals

Temporal Nature of Goal	Goal
Short-Term/Immediate Goal	Pete has the goal of getting a good grade on this Friday's vocabulary test.
Long-Term/Distant Goal	Emma has the goal of going to medical school.
Ongoing Goal	Cody has the goal of practicing the violin at least five days per week.

These goals probably seem like typical academic goals that many students might have for themselves. But is having a goal sufficient? If a student has a goal, is that enough for the student to eventually achieve the goal? The simple answer is "no!" Goals help to direct our motivation, but a goal in and of itself is not sufficient; most of us need something more than just a goal. Without looking ahead, write down a few thoughts about what each of the students mentioned above (Pete, Emma, and Cody) would also need to do in order to achieve their goals.

Now refer to Table 1.4, which includes some possible actions that each student could take in order to achieve his or her goal. Some of the strategies that you suggested may be similar to those that are presented in Table 1.4. These are just examples, of course; there are many strategies that these students can implement in order to achieve their goals.

Hopefully you are beginning to see that there is more to a goal than just having a "goal." Think about dieting or exercise; most of us from time to time set a personal goal for dieting or exercising; but is the goal enough? Is it enough to just tell yourself that you will exercise every day, or is something else required?

Goals are important, but we can only accomplish our goals if we (a) know what we need to do to accomplish the goal, and (b) have confidence that we can successfully carry out the steps required to accomplish the goal. You may have a goal of exercising five times per week, but to succeed, you would need to know how to fit exercising into your schedule, and you would need to have the confidence that you could manage to keep

Table 1.4 Strategies for Accomplishing Academic Goals

Temporal Nature of Goal	Goal	Some Actions the Student Could Take to Achieve the Goal
Short-Term/Immediate Goal	Pete has the goal of getting a good grade on this Friday's vocabulary test.	• Study every night this week • Get a good night's sleep on Thursday
Long-Term/Distant Goal	Emma has the goal of going to medical school.	• Get good grades throughout high school • Get accepted into college, major in biology, and get good grades
Ongoing Goal	Cody has the goal of practicing playing the violin at least five days per week.	• Organize his homework and other responsibilities so that he has enough time to practice every night.

that schedule. Pete may have the goal of getting a good grade on Friday's vocabulary test, but he will only achieve that goal if he knows what he needs to do to prepare for the test, and if he has the confidence that he can do what is needed.

You have now learned another important lesson about student motivation: *Students' goals affect their motivation, but goals in and of themselves are not sufficient.* As a classroom teacher, you have the opportunity to support your students as they strive to achieve their goals. In later chapters, we will discuss in greater depth the strategies that you as a teacher can use to help your students to (a) set reasonable goals, (b) consider what they will need to do in order to achieve those goals, and (c) develop sustained confidence as they work toward achieving those goals.

Intrinsic and Extrinsic Motivation

There is one additional aspect of motivation that we need to consider before we begin to explore the ways in which you, as a teacher, can positively influence your students' motivation. Specifically, there is a distinction between *intrinsic* and *extrinsic* motivation. Although there is much theory and research that examines the sources and consequences of intrinsic and extrinsic motivation (e.g., Deci & Ryan, 2012), for now let's just look at what each of these means on a general level. A student is **intrinsically motivated** to engage with a particular task when the student wants to engage with the task simply because the student likes the task. Intrinsically motivated students engage with tasks because they want to; they often become deeply engrossed in the task and often don't care if they spend a great deal of time on the task. In contrast, a student is **extrinsically motivated** to engage with a particular task when the student engages with the task either to obtain a reward (e.g., a good grade or a prize) or to avoid a negative consequence (e.g., being reprimanded by the teacher). Extrinsically motivated students engage with tasks because the task is a means to an end; they often (but not always) do not want to spend a great deal of time on the task—just enough so that they can obtain a reward or avoid a penalty. Let's look at a few examples; decide if each of these students is intrinsically or extrinsically motivated:

- Amy loves painting—it's her favorite hobby at home when she has free time.

- Maia is fascinated by science and loves to learn all that she can about it.

- Alex practices his cello every day, because his parents give him $10.00 per week if he practices for at least 20 minutes per day.

- Rick works very hard to make sure he gets As in all of his classes because he knows that if he has a straight A average, he might be able to get accepted into his dream college.

Amy and Maia are *intrinsically motivated*. Amy paints because she enjoys painting, and Maia likes to study science because she finds it interesting. In contrast, Alex and Rick are *extrinsically motivated*; Alex practices his cello simply because he knows he'll get $10.00 at the end of the week if he does so daily; and Rick works very hard to get As because he knows that a transcript filled with As will help him to get accepted to his favored college.

Now take a moment to think a bit more about these students. Amy and Maia are intrinsically motivated, but could they also be extrinsically motivated? Alex and Rick are extrinsically motivated, but could they also be intrinsically motivated? The answers to both questions are *yes*! Intrinsic and extrinsic motivation are often thought of as opposite ends of a continuum when in fact they are entirely separate aspects of motivation.

For example, although Amy is intrinsically motivated to paint, she also could be extrinsically motivated to paint; perhaps she wants to attend art school someday, with the understanding that she needs to have a portfolio of outstanding examples of her work in order to get admitted to art school. She is intrinsically motivated to paint because she enjoys painting, but she could be extrinsically motivated to paint in order to get into school.

In later chapters, we will introduce strategies that will help you to encourage intrinsic motivation. We'll also be realistic and acknowledge that the world is filled with extrinsic incentives and penalties. Therefore, we'll also introduce strategies that will show you how to acknowledge and use extrinsic incentives in ways that do not harm students' intrinsic motivation.

 STRATEGY 1.3

Intrinsic or Extrinsic?

Are your students intrinsically motivated, extrinsically motivated, or both? Here is a simple strategy that you can use to assess your students' motivation:

Suppose that you are teaching a unit on long division. Ask your students to anonymously write down the answer to this question: *"Why are you learning how to do long division?"* You might want to give them some prompts: *"There are many reasons as to why people learn how to do long division; I'm curious about what you think about this. For example, some students believe we learn long division because it will be helpful to us in our future jobs; some students believe we learn long division because we will be tested on it; and some students believe we learn long division because it is fun to do. Why do you think that we are learning long division? There are no right or wrong answers. Write down all of the reasons why you think that you are learning long division."*

By asking your students to respond anonymously, it will encourage them to be honest with you. Look through their responses. This will give you an insight into whether your students are approaching the study of long division with intrinsic motivation, extrinsic motivation, or a combination of both intrinsic and extrinsic motivation.

MOTIVATION MYTH

Myth: *For any given academic task, a student can either be intrinsically motivated (i.e., the student wants to engage with the task because it is interesting) or extrinsically motivated (i.e., the student engages with the task because it is required or the student will be tested on aspects of the task), but not both.*

Truth: *For any task, a student can have many different combinations of intrinsic and extrinsic motivation. For example, Susan might really enjoy writing book reports (high intrinsic motivation) and also work hard at writing book reports to get a good grade (high extrinsic); Jimmy might find writing book reports very boring (low intrinsic) but still work hard on writing reports to get a good grade (high extrinsic).*

Revisiting Our Definition of Motivation

Earlier in this chapter, we noted that there are many textbook definitions of motivation. Hopefully at this point you are beginning to realize that the word "motivation" is a catchall term that encompasses several factors. In this book, we are going to approach motivation by thinking of it as consisting of a series of processes, *all of which can be impacted by teachers*. In this book, academic motivation is defined broadly:

> *Academic motivation is a process that explains why students engage in specific activities throughout their education. Students' motivation is determined by their needs, their beliefs, and their goals (i.e., the sources of their motivation). Moreover, student motivation can be intrinsic (i.e., engaging in activities because we simply enjoy doing them), or extrinsic (i.e., engaging in activities because we will get something in return for participating).*

As we explore the ways that you as a teacher can positively impact student motivation, keep in mind that your students' motivation may be a bit more complex than you may have originally thought (prior to reading this chapter). For any academic task that your students are working on, your students' motivation to master a learning goal may be influenced by several factors such as their goals for the day, their beliefs about the value of the task, etc. Moreover, their motivation to learn something new may be intrinsic (that is, they really want to engage with the task because they are enjoying the experience) or extrinsic (namely, they are engaging with the task because they know they will be graded on their performance). Or their motivation could be some combination of intrinsic and extrinsic, if they are engaging with the task because it is fun, but they also are working hard at it because they know they will receive a grade.

Summing Up

This chapter provided an introduction to student motivation. Motivation is influenced by students' needs, beliefs, and goals. These needs, beliefs, and goals can have both positive and detrimental effects on student motivation. In addition, a student's motivation in any given situation might be intrinsic—such as when the student is working on an assignment because it's really interesting and fun; extrinsic—namely when the student is working on an assignment because it will be graded; or both—that is, the assignment might be interesting, but the student also is very aware of the fact that it will be graded. When we as teachers are aware of the various processes that influence our students' motivation, we are better able to design lessons and adjust our instruction so that we can help all of our students to become motivated learners.

☀ APPLYING WHAT YOU HAVE LEARNED

Let's start using some of what you have learned in this chapter. Think about the components of motivation that we discussed in this chapter (needs, beliefs, and goals). Now, think about a particular time in your life when you were not motivated, such as in an academic setting. At that specific time, what were your needs? What were your beliefs and goals relative to the topic being studied? Would you characterize your motivation at the time as being intrinsic, extrinsic, or both?

Next, if you are a practicing (or former) teacher, try to think about how needs, beliefs, and goals play roles in your students' motivation. Try to think about a specific student that you teach (either one who is highly motivated or one who is not highly motivated). Do you have a sense of that student's needs, beliefs, and goals? If not, would it have been helpful to you to be aware of them?

Finally, think about what you may have learned about your motivation and the student's motivation by doing this exercise. Perhaps you are beginning to see that motivation is not straightforward! There are many processes and thoughts at play simultaneously, and all of these affect motivation. In the next chapter, we'll begin to look at this in more depth with an eye toward the roles of the student, the teacher, and parents in shaping student motivation.

WHO SHAPES STUDENT MOTIVATION?

CHAPTER

2

In this chapter, we're going to start to examine the sources of your students' motivation. Whether a student is highly motivated or completely unmotivated, it's natural for us to consider the reasons for our students' high (or low) motivation. Let's consider two examples; in each of these examples, a teacher has written comments on students' first-semester report cards. These are the comments:

(1) Neal, Grade 5. "*Neal does not seem to be very motivated in class. He often does not pay attention. He is easily distracted and often starts to chat with others. He often does not complete his homework, and he does not seem to study for tests.*"

(2) Carrie, Grade 5. "*Carrie is one of the most motivated students in class. She is always eager to learn. She finishes her work quickly and accurately, and she is very well behaved. She always seems to be paying very close attention to what we are working on in class. She loves to learn!*"

You can probably quite accurately predict the reactions that Neal's and Carrie's parents will have after reading these comments; Neal's parents will probably be quite concerned, while Carrie's parents probably will feel quite proud.

But for both Neal and Carrie, an important question looms in the background: Who is responsible for Carrie's seemingly high motivation and for Neal's low motivation? As you'll start to see throughout this chapter, this is a vital question that often is ignored; nevertheless, it is extremely important to consider this question, if we want to ensure that all students are optimally motivated to learn.

Understanding Your Own Motivation

In this chapter, we're going to explore some of the factors that impact our students' motivation. But before we do that, let's first take a look at some of the factors that influence our own motivation. When you think about your own motivation—that is, motivation toward your job, toward academic pursuits, toward leisure activities, and so forth—what causes you to be motivated (i.e., what determines your motivation)? Is your motivation primarily determined by internal factors such as your personality, your abilities, your priorities, your likes, and dislikes, or is your motivation determined by external factors like family concerns, societal norms, your supervisor's expectations, and so forth? Or is your motivation perhaps determined by both internal and external factors?

YOUR PERSONALITY AND YOUR MOTIVATION

Let's start our examination of influences on your motivation by discussing the concept of **personality**. Have you ever thought about how you would describe your personality? Do you think that aspects of your personality affect your motivation? Let's explore this in the following activity.

- First, think about your personality. If you had to list <u>five</u> of your personality traits, what would they be? (Think very broadly about personality traits; we're not looking for scientific precision in your responses). Some of these traits might be: *shy, outgoing, dependent, confident, anxious, helpful, hard-working, pessimistic, responsible, creative*, and so forth. Write these five traits down in the Activity 2.1 chart.

- Next, think about some *activity or task that you are motivated do regularly* (e.g., something that you have to do repeatedly at your job; taking care of your children; paying bills; etc.); don't worry about the type of motivation that you have for the activity right now (e.g., intrinsic, extrinsic, etc.); just think about the activity itself. Write down a very brief description of this activity in the top row of the Activity 2.1 chart.

- Write down what time it is right now: _____

- Now, next to each of the five personality traits that you listed, write a sentence or two describing how each of these aspects of your personality impacts your motivation to do the activity that you just identified. **Don't proceed to the next step until you finish this part!**

- Write down what time it is right now (immediately after writing your descriptive sentences): _____

- Finally, select which of the following statements best describes how you felt while you were doing this activity:
  (a) It was very easy.
  (b) It was a bit harder than I thought it might be; although a few of my personality traits were easy to connect to the activity, I had to think a bit about some of the others.
  (c) It was much harder than I thought it might be; the connections between most of the personality traits and the activity weren't as obvious as I initially thought that they would be.
  (d) It was very difficult, and I gave up.

Activity 2.1 Personality and Motivation

What is a task or activity that you are motivated to do regularly?

Personality Trait	Relationship of Personality Trait to the Task That You Do Regularly
Activity:	
1.	
2.	
3.	
4.	
5.	

Now, let's examine your responses. First, think about your response to the final question (about how you felt during the activity). If I were going to bet, I would bet that you probably selected "b" or "c" as your response. For most of us, this is not an overwhelmingly difficult activity, but it isn't simple either. The connections between aspects of our personalities and our motivation are not always obvious; moreover, sometimes, there simply is no obvious connection between our personality traits and our own motivation.

Next, look at the two times that you wrote down, and calculate how many minutes it took you to come up with the five connections between your personality traits and the task. Did this take longer than you expected? For many of us, it takes more time than we realized to complete an activity of this nature; this is because *personality variables are in fact only one of many different kinds of variables that are responsible for our motivation.* It often is difficult for us to identify specific connections between our personality traits and our motivated behaviors, because our personality is just one of the many variables that influence our motivation. Moreover, some of our personality traits are unrelated to some of our motivated behaviors. *(As a personal example, one aspect of my job as a college professor is teaching, which I do regularly and I enjoy. Nevertheless, I have always considered myself to be an introvert; when I think about teaching, there is no obvious connection between my self-perception as an introvert and my positive motivation toward teaching [and I actually tend to be quite outgoing when I'm teaching – no signs of introversion!] Although introversion is part of my personality, other variables in my life seem to take precedence in my motivation to teach; my tendency toward introversion is real, but it has no obvious effect on my teaching).*

Students' Personalities

Have you ever taken a personality assessment, like the *Myers-Briggs*? Or a personality test that is available for free on the Internet? Many of us have taken these assessments, often as part of our jobs. These "tests" provide information geared toward helping us to better understand how our personalities shape our motivation.

While these tests are quite popular among employers and are often used in higher education and work settings, there is much debate about whether or not they actually provide meaningful information (Hunsley, Lee, & Wood, 2003). Nevertheless, the *prevalence* of assessments like the *Myers-Briggs* perpetrates a societal message about the importance of personality variables as determinants of our motivation. If you ever took the *Myers-Briggs* (or a similar assessment), did you come away from the experience believing that the results must be important? Does your employer believe that the results are important?

I'm not questioning whether or not the results are important; but what I do hope that you are beginning to see is that there are many individuals in our society who greatly value personality indicators of this nature. Hopefully, the activity that you just completed demonstrated to you that while there certainly are some connections between personality characteristics and motivation, your personality does not completely explain why you are motivated to do what you do (e.g., at work, at school, at home, etc.). As we will see throughout this chapter, there also are other variables that influence your motivation, in addition to your personality.

RE-EXAMINING OUR DEFINITION OF MOTIVATION IN LIGHT OF PERSONALITY

Before we look at some of the other factors that influence motivation, let's return to the definition of academic motivation from Chapter 1. As you may recall, we defined academic motivation in terms of our students' **needs, beliefs,** and **goals**. Are needs, beliefs, and goals parts of our personalities? They certainly are *influenced by our personalities*, but they also are influenced by many other factors as well. "Personality" was not even part of our definition of motivation!

It's important to keep this in mind, so that as teachers, we don't fall into the trap of thinking that our students' personality traits are the primary determinants of their motivation. If you ever took an introductory psychology course, you probably learned that all humans have a tendency toward believing that personality traits are major determinants of behaviors; this is referred to as the **fundamental attribution error** (Ross, 2018). As teachers, we need to be careful not to assume that our students' personality traits are the most important determinants of their motivation in school. It's easy for us to characterize our students based on a few simple adjectives (e.g., "she's lazy"; "he's a troublemaker"). We need to remind ourselves that there are many influences on our students' motivation—more than just the personality traits that you observe. In the next few sections, we'll look at some of those other influences.

 STRATEGY 2.1

The Fundamental Attribution Error

Do you, perhaps unintentionally, assume that some of your students' personality traits determine their motivation? The following strategy may help you to think more broadly about what motivates your students:

(Continued)

(Continued)

Once per month, spend a few minutes going through your class lists and briefly thinking about each student's academic motivation. Specifically, try to do the following for each student:

1. Consider the students' motivation in your classroom (don't think about this too much . . . just your general impressions of their motivation at this time).

2. Next ask yourself why you came to that conclusion . . . Why is this student motivated in a particular way at this moment in time?

Now look at your conclusions for each of your students. You might be surprised to see that you are committing the fundamental attribution error—you may be focusing solely on aspects of the students' personalities (e.g., "she's lazy"; "he doesn't listen"; "she is smart") rather than also acknowledging that there may be other variables at play. Taking the time to check ourselves in this way helps us to remember that our students' personalities are not the sole determinants of their motivation.

Teachers

Most of this book is about how teachers affect student motivation. Therefore, I'm only going to briefly mention the influence of teachers in this chapter (because the rest of the book is about teachers), simply to acknowledge that teachers' behaviors and beliefs are extremely important determinants of student motivation. Nevertheless, if as teachers we want to positively influence our students' motivation, we need to recognize and acknowledge other factors that impact student motivation.

Table 2.1 includes a list of some of the many ways that teachers impact student motivation. Note that this table includes a list of various examples of both teacher behaviors and teacher beliefs. We will explore the specific effects of each of these behaviors and beliefs throughout the remaining chapters. The purpose here is simply to introduce these to you, so that you can begin to see that as a teacher, your behaviors and beliefs are one of several factors that influence students' motivation.

Table 2.1 Examples of Teacher Influences on Student Motivation

Type of Teacher Influence	Description of Influence on Motivation
Teacher Behaviors	Quality and quantity of **feedback** provided on assignments, projects, or tests.
	The types of **assignments** that teachers provide.
	The ways that teachers **present** new information.
	The types of **assessments** that are used.
	The ways that teachers **manage behavior**.
	The **instructional strategies** used on a daily basis.
	The ways that teachers **recognize** students' effort and achievement.
	The ways that teachers **group** students for learning activities.
	The amount of **autonomy** (independence) that students are afforded.
	The types of interpersonal **relationships** that teachers develop with students.
Teacher Beliefs	Teachers' **beliefs about students' abilities**.
	Teachers' **expectations** (i.e., expectations for individual students' academic performance).
	Teachers' **individual efficacy beliefs** (i.e., the belief that as a teacher, you can successfully teach and support your students' learning needs).
	Teachers' **collective efficacy beliefs** (i.e., the beliefs of a group of teachers in the school regarding their combined ability to teach effectively and support student learning)
	Teachers' beliefs regarding the **support** that they receive from **school administrators**.

Parents

Think about your childhood and your adolescence. How did your parents or guardians influence your motivation? Did they influence your daily motivation to do your homework and to study? Did they influence your longer-term motivation (e.g., motivation to go to college)? Did they influence your life choices and your current career path? You probably answered "yes" to all of these questions.

Parents[1] do influence their children's motivation. However, their influence is broad. Parents impact students' current motivation (e.g., whether or not they do their homework each night), as well as their long-term motivation (e.g., whether or not they pursue postsecondary education). Consequently, your students' personality traits are not the only influences on their motivation—parents also affect their motivation. As a teacher, it is important to understand the roles that parents play in impacting your students' motivation.

PARENTAL INFLUENCES ON STUDENTS' MOTIVATION

Let's review some of the ways that parents influence students' motivation and specifically why these findings are relevant to you as a classroom teacher.

Parenting Styles

The ways that parents interact with children and adolescents have effects on academic motivation and achievement. There are many ways to talk about parental interactions. In Table 2.2, I present a rubric that has been well documented in the literature and that has implications for student motivation.

As you can see, the *authoritative style* of parenting is the one that has the most positive effects on students' achievement and motivation. An authoritative parent is one who both (a) allows and encourages children to become independent and to make decisions, but simultaneously (b) has high expectations and sets very clear boundaries about what is and is not acceptable. In contrast, the rejecting/neglecting style is often predictive of students experiencing both social and academic problems (e.g., misbehaving and not getting good grades).

Nevertheless, it's important to note that while these parenting styles have been identified by many researchers, there is much variation in how parenting occurs within any given family. It is certainly possible that a parent may for the most part have an authoritative parenting style, but also may be somewhat permissive at times. It also is important to acknowledge that there are cultural differences in parenting styles. For example, some parents may be very strict and demanding, but also are so in

---

[1]The term "parents" will be used throughout this book for ease of presentation. However, it is important to acknowledge that our students can have a wide range of parents, guardians, and caretakers.

Table 2.2 Parenting Styles

Style	Description	Example	Effects on Motivation and Achievement
Authoritative	These parents tend to have high academic and behavioral expectations, while also encouraging their children to make responsible decisions and to understand the consequences of those decisions.	Liam is a seventh grader. His parents encourage him to decide each evening when and how he will complete his homework; but there is a clear expectation that homework must be completed every night.	On average, these students do well in school, value effort, and use appropriate social skills with their peers.
Authoritarian	These parents have high academic and behavioral expectations; they also are quite controlling and do not encourage independent decision-making.	Chantoya is a fourth grader. Her parents expect her to work hard on her studies and to behave well in school and at home. Chantoya is on a strict schedule after school—she must complete all of her homework before she can do anything else (e.g., watch TV, play with a friend).	On average, these students are not as academically successful as are students with authoritative parents. They may be somewhat insecure and lack confidence.
Permissive	These parents are emotionally close to their children; however, they set few rules and limitations on behavior.	Ethan is an eleventh grader. He has a great relationship with his mom and dad. There are no formal rules in place regarding what Ethan should be doing after school or in the evenings; he can more or less do whatever he wants to do.	On average, these students may be more likely to misbehave and be off task. They often succumb to peer pressure and may be immature compared to their peers.
Rejecting/ Neglecting	These parents are not very involved with their children. They tend not to have close, warm relationships.	Darcy is a sixth grader. Her parents do not pay much attention to Darcy's schoolwork and are usually not aware of whether she has homework or a test coming up. Darcy does not get hugged very often, and she does not feel like she can talk to her parents about social or academic issues.	On average, these students do not do well in school and often experience social problems as well.

Developed using the following sources: Baumrind (1991, 2005); Gray & Steinberg (1999); Laursen & Collins (2009).

a very loving, caring manner. Moreover, parents may want and need to be particularly strict with their children in order to assure their safety when the family lives in high-crime neighborhoods (Leyendecker, Harwood, Comparini, & Yalçinkaya, 2005).

As a classroom teacher, you need to acknowledge that these parenting styles do exist and that they are one of the many factors that influence your students' motivation and learning. You may not be able to do anything to change a parent's style of parenting, but when you understand that these parental influences exist and have real effects on your students, it may affect how you interact with and support your students. And remember the fundamental attribution error—as teachers, we may be prone to assuming that our students' motivation is fully under their own control. Whereas our students certainly do have control, parental influences are very real, and your recognition and acknowledgement of these influences may help you to better understand your students and to develop better relationships with them (a topic which we will explore in depth in Chapter 7).

Activity 2.2 Parenting Styles

What parenting styles did your parents have? Using the four styles described in Table 2.2, try to identify the parenting style(s) of your parents or guardians. Keep in mind that if you lived in a two-parent household, both parents might not always have the same style. In addition, their styles might have changed over time. Write a few sentences reflecting on this. Then, using the information provided in the last column of Table 2.2, briefly reflect on how your parents' styles might have affected your motivation and achievement.

PARENT INVOLVEMENT IN ACADEMICS

As a teacher, you probably often hear from your colleagues, from administrators, from the PTA, and from others about the importance of parent involvement. There is a widespread assumption that parent involvement is universally beneficial to students and will support student motivation. Whereas this is generally true, we have to ask ourselves, *"What does parent involvement truly mean?"* Does **involvement** mean physically being present in the classroom several times per week volunteering? Does it mean attending parent-teacher conferences? Does it mean helping students with homework? Does it mean chaperoning a field trip?

Well, it means all of the above. It's important to understand that some parents have the time and resources to be involved at school (i.e., to be physically in the school building), whereas others don't. Some parents have to work several jobs to support their families, and whereas they might want to be more involved at school, life circumstances may prevent this.

Given these variations in what parents can reasonably do, there are some robust research findings regarding the relationships between certain types of parent involvement and motivation. Table 2.3 contains recommendations for parental behaviors that can support student motivation. As a teacher, you may be able to support and promote some of these behaviors from time to time.

You'll note that I am conceptualizing "involvement" very broadly. In addition to what you might think of as traditional types of parent involvement (e.g., volunteering in the classroom or attending a parent-teacher conference), parents also are involved with regard to how they monitor homework, how much they value education, and how much they encourage autonomy. And although there is often a stereotype that fathers' involvement is not as important as mothers' involvement, research suggests that involvement of fathers can have the same positive effects as mothers' involvement (Kim & Hill, 2015).

The positive effects of parent involvement are not always uniform across all families. For example, although parent involvement in their children's academic pursuits is related to student academic success, parental involvement has stronger effects when parents feel efficacious and interested in the subject area

Table 2.3 Recommendations for How Parental Involvement Can Promote Students' Motivation

Parent Belief/Behavior	Effects on Students
Parents should support students' autonomy (i.e., allow children to have greater independence and to take on more responsibility as they get older).	Higher achievement, more autonomous motivation, and greater psychological well-being.
Parents should believe in and regularly talk about the importance of education.	Higher achievement, particularly when parents encourage their children to focus on and prioritize academic work.
Parents should hold high academic expectations. They should believe that their children are academically competent, and communicate that belief.	When parents express confidence in their children, this reinforces the importance of students' continuing to exert effort and to prioritize academics. However, when parents see that a child is struggling, the parents need to work with teachers to provide resources (e.g., perhaps tutoring) so that the student can succeed; parents can still show their confidence as the child makes progress with this extra support.
Parents should expect that homework is completed, and they should provide time and support at home so that students can prioritize their homework.	Higher achievement

Developed using the following sources: Grolnick, Lerner, Raftery-Helmer, & Allen (2020); Jodl et al. (2001); Patall & Zambrano (2019); Simpkins, Fredricks J.A., & Eccles, J.S. (2012); Vasquez, Patall, Fong, Corrigan, & Pine (2016).

(Häfner et al., 2018). Parents who feel confident about helping their children with algebra homework or who display a great interest in math have a bit of an advantage over parents who do not feel confident or who are not as interested in math. But this does not mean that children whose parents are not interested in or do not feel efficacious about math are going to do poorly in math! As teachers, we simply need to be aware that we can't expect that all of our students' parents will be able to provide adequate academic support at all times, for all assignments.

STRATEGY 2.2
Getting Parents Involved

What strategies do you use to encourage parent involvement? Below I describe a relatively easy way to encourage parental involvement aimed at enhancing students' motivation.

Sometimes parents want to be involved, but don't know exactly what they should do. This is particularly true for parents of adolescents. In your communications with parents (e.g., via an email message, a handout that students bring home, or even during parent-teacher meetings or "meet the teacher" events), you can offer suggestions for some ways that parents can be involved (with the goal of supporting student motivation). Here are some strategies you might suggest to parents:

- Encourage your child to come up with a plan for how to accomplish nightly homework; allow your child to try the plan, then talk about how effective it was, and revise the plan as needed.

- Regularly communicate to your child that you believe in the value of education.

- Express confidence in your child's academic abilities.

- Ask your child about what s/he is learning about in a particular subject area (e.g., perhaps at the dinner table, ask what the child is learning about right now in social studies).

- Hold high (but reasonable) expectations for academic performance; when your child is not doing well academically, don't get angry—try to talk about the support that your child might need.

- Help your child to allocate time to complete homework each night.

- Reach out to me at any time. I am here to help— by phone, by email, Zoom or Skype, in person, or whatever works best for you.

We of course need to acknowledge that not all of our students' parents will be able to implement these suggestions; your suggestions for parents need to be tactful, practical, respectful, and culturally appropriate.

Schools

As teachers, most of us think about how we as individuals affect our students' motivation. But we also need to recognize that the school as a whole also influences student motivation. Let's do an exercise to explore this. All schools have policies—policies related to student attendance, to behavior, to tardiness, to bullying—and to many other aspects of school life. Think about the school where you teach (or any school, if you aren't currently teaching) and write down the first five policies that you can think of in the left-hand column of Activity 2.3—but keep in mind that these must be *school-level policies*, not policies that you as a teacher may have set for your individual classroom. Next, in the right column, write a few words describing how this policy might affect student motivation.

Activity 2.3 School Policies and Student Motivation

Policy	Impact on Motivation
1.	
2.	
3.	
4.	
5.	

Are you struggling a bit with this activity? If you are, here is a clue: You may need to think broadly about this—some school policies might affect motivation related to taking tests; some policies might affect students' motivation to pay attention and stay on task; and some policies might influence motivation related to good behavior. Moreover, school-level policies may not affect all students in the same way—some policies might affect motivation in older students but not younger ones or in male students but not female students. So, if you are experiencing some difficulty relating the policies that you identified to your students' motivation, don't give up—spend some time really thinking about each of these policies and try to force yourself to see some possible connections!

Once you are finished, think about the connections that you drew between school-level policies and student motivation. Were you surprised to find that when you were pushed to really think about the motivational implications of school policies, there are in fact connections between policy and motivation that you had not considered before? A nice follow-up to this activity is to show your responses to this exercise to a colleague at your school and to ask for your colleague's thoughts about the policies that you identified and how your colleague sees those policies affecting student motivation in your school. You'll probably be surprised that some of your colleagues will immediately agree with the connections that you have made between the policies and motivation, whereas others will see entirely different connections of the policies to motivation.

SCHOOL POLICIES AND STUDENT MOTIVATION

As you probably recognized from this exercise, school-level policies do influence student learning and motivation (Maehr & Midgley, 1991). Let's look at a few examples of how some rather common school-level policies might impact motivation.

- In Freemont Middle School, the "A" honor roll is displayed on the main bulletin board by the school entrance; every student and teacher must walk past the honor roll several times per day. Cindy, who is failing most of her classes, feels upset every time she passes by the honor roll—although it's posted there to motivate students, seeing it just makes her angry. Cindy feels like she'll never make the honor roll, and she doesn't like seeing it all the time.

- In Hawthorne Elementary School, students are forbidden to chew gum. The school policy about gum chewing is very strict—anyone who is caught chewing gum will get sent to the principal's office— no exceptions! Jordan, who is in third grade and is a very responsible student, walked into school one day chewing gum—he honestly just forgot that he had the gum in his mouth. His teacher noticed this and immediately sent him to the principal's office (Jordan had never gotten in trouble before). Jordan broke down in tears and was very upset that he was being sent to the principal's office; all of the other students saw that Jordan was in trouble, and he was very embarrassed. The next day, Jordan pretended to feel sick so he could stay home from school.

- In Jefferson High School, students may only enroll in honors classes if a teacher recommends and approves of the enrollment. Jennifer really loves biology and hopes to become a doctor. She wants to take Honors Biology next year, but her previous science teacher did not think she would be successful in the class, and refused to grant permission for Jennifer to enroll. Jennifer infers from this that she must not be as good at science as she had thought that she was, and her interest in biology declines.

- At Silverwood High School, students are allowed to retake math tests as often as they want to. Jillian got a C on her algebra quiz on quadratic equations, but because of the retake policy, she kept practicing solving quadratic equations, and retook the test twice, earning a B the second time and an A the third time.

Each of the school policies described in these examples is well intentioned; I can't think of any school personnel that I have ever encountered who would deliberately implement a strategy that would be harmful to students. Nevertheless, these examples all demonstrate that these policies, while well intentioned, may benefit some students and backfire with others. The policy regarding honors classes at Jefferson High was put in place to ensure that students are enrolling in classes where they will be successful; nevertheless, the policy had a detrimental effect on Jennifer's motivation because it prevented her from pursuing her interest in biology. The gum-chewing policy at Hawthorne Elementary was implemented because teachers and administrators believe that chewing gum distracts students from learning; nevertheless, Jordan's unintentional forgetfulness caused him to experience great distress and led him to pretend to be sick and to miss an entire day of school. The test retake policy at Silverwood High School fulfilled its intended purpose with Jillian—instead of giving up and accepting a C grade on her math test, she was motivated to work harder, and she eventually both earned an A grade and mastered solving quadratic equations.

However, each of these policies could just as easily have produced other outcomes with different students. Whereas Jillian took advantage of the test retake policy and benefited from it, other students might not care about such a policy and decide not to bother retaking an exam. And whereas the gum-chewing policy led to a great deal of anxiety for Jordan, the prohibition of gum probably does help some students to concentrate on their work.

The key message from these examples is that **school policies do affect student motivation—both positively and negatively**. When educators implement schoolwide policies, it is important to consider both the intended and potential unintended effects that the policies might have on our students. As a classroom teacher, you are certainly most focused on your own classroom and your own efforts to motivate your students; but in the background, larger schoolwide policies do affect student motivation. You need to keep these school policies in mind and always consider how the strategies that you implement in your classroom align (or don't align) with larger school-level policies.

STRATEGY 2.3
The Honor Roll

Does the school that you work at have an honor roll? What are the criteria for a student to be on the honor roll? Does the honor roll truly serve as a motivator for students at your school?

Honor rolls are well intentioned, and are designed to encourage students to work hard. But sometimes having an honor roll can backfire, because some students may feel that they will never be able to get even close to being on the honor roll; these students may feel that the school only values the highest achieving students (particularly if only the "A" students can get on the honor roll). Try to initiate a discussion of the purpose of the honor roll with your colleagues. You might want to discuss the effectiveness of the honor roll with a few other teachers at first, and then perhaps speak to a school administrator about having a faculty-wide discussion about the honor roll.

Try to truly have a critical discussion about the honor roll—many of your colleagues will adamantly defend the importance of having an honor roll . . . but try to really get everyone to think about this and look at it from the perspectives of low-achieving students. You might even want to ask some students to (anonymously) write down their feelings about the honor roll and then share those with your colleagues. They might be surprised at some of the students' responses.

An alternative to traditional "A" honor rolls is an "improvement" honor roll. Students earn a place on the honor roll if they demonstrate improvement. Many students, parents, and educators don't like the idea of an improvement-based honor roll; they argue that once a student gets an A, the student can't improve. I don't buy this argument—I always say "A stands for artificial." Even students who have earned As can improve; it all depends on how one defines improvement. From a motivation perspective, the honor roll can motivate any student—because any student can improve. But one has to question whether a student who is barely passing any classes would be motivated by an "A" honor roll.

MOTIVATION MYTH

Myth: *School-level policies don't really affect motivation; it's really all about the students' attitudes.*

Truth: *Policies implemented at the school level often do affect student motivation. Policies are almost always well intentioned, but the potential effects of the policies on all students in the school must be carefully considered.*

Communities, Neighborhoods, and Society

Was your motivation influenced by the neighborhood in which you grew up? For most of us, the answer is "yes." Students' motivation is affected by both people and policies in their immediate surroundings (i.e., their parents and their schools), as well as broader social contexts (e.g., neighborhoods) (Garner & Raudenbush, 1991; Whitaker, Graham, Severtson, Furr-Holden, & Latimer, 2012).

COMMUNITIES AND NEIGHBORHOODS

Although as teachers we often don't think about it, the larger social contexts of our students' lives affect their academic motivation. For example, there is a relationship between the economic well-being of neighborhoods and student academic success: Students who reside in more affluent communities on average achieve greater academic successes than do students who reside in socioeconomically disadvantaged neighborhoods (McLoyd et al., 2009; Whitaker et al., 2012). This is partially explained by the fact that families that reside in more affluent neighborhoods often have the financial means to provide children (and adolescents) with resources that support learning and motivation. More affluent families may be able to have more books available in the home and may be able to spend more time reading with young children (Barnes & Puccioni, 2017). It is important for us to be aware of these inequities. For example, children who have had extensive early literacy experiences transition into kindergarten with stronger academic preparation than do children who have not been exposed to as many books or to reading; children who have had this exposure may enter school with greater academic motivation

(Diamond, Justice, Siegler, Snyder, & National Center for Special Education Research, 2013). The students who have not had many literacy experiences may in some cases never catch up to their peers; this obviously has long-term effects on their achievement, their motivation, and their future educational and professional opportunities.

The values and traditions of communities also impact student motivation (Eccles & Roeser, 2011). When children and adolescents reside in communities in which few students enroll in postsecondary education, motivation to attend college may not be high. For example, if students live in rural communities in which most families work on farms or in coal mines, traditional family and community norms might be for youth to continue with the family tradition and to work on the farms or in the coal mines after completing high school (Anderman et al., 2002). Attending college may not be a high priority for students in such a community.

If you currently teach, think about the neighborhoods/communities where your current students reside. How might each of the following neighborhood characteristics affect your students' motivation?

- Average family household income
- The graduation rate of your local high school
- The political makeup of the community (i.e., is this a highly conservative community? a highly liberal community?)
- Cultural and religious backgrounds of families
- Location of the community (i.e., urban, rural, or suburban)

This is a tricky question; it's very easy to think about this question and to view the majority of our students vis a vis stereotypes about the communities in which we work (e.g., "it's a poor community"; "everyone goes to college"; etc.). As educators, we need to establish a balance between (a) being knowledgeable about the social contexts of the communities in which we teach and (b) avoiding strict adherence to stereotypes about the students who attend our schools. Moreover, we need to recognize that there is a tremendous amount of variation in the students with whom we work; long-held stereotypes about the community may reflect reality for some students, but certainly not for all of our students.

Let's look at an example. Kevin Morgan teaches in a school district characterized by above-average high school dropout rates. Whereas Kevin could embrace this statistic and look at all of his students as potential dropouts, Kevin recognizes that the higher-than-average dropout rate does not reflect upon all of the students at his school. Rather than seeing this as a deficit in the students or the community, Kevin recognizes that as a teacher, he needs to understand that there is a high dropout rate in the community and that this knowledge empowers him to work with his colleagues to try to figure out why the rates are high and to work toward solutions.

SOCIETAL INFLUENCES

Academic motivation is also affected by broader social contexts. Our students regularly see and hear messages that affect their motivation; these messages may come from friends and family, from television shows and movies and social media, from advertisements, and from numerous other sources. For example, there was widespread publicity in the early 1990s about a talking Barbie® doll; one of the sentences that talking Barbie could say was, "*Math class is tough*" (*New York Times*, October 21, 1992). After complaints were raised about the message that this sends about math (particularly to girls), the manufacturer of talking Barbie removed this statement from Barbie's vocabulary. Messages of this nature, which are out of teachers' control, can affect our students' motivation. A teacher may work very hard at helping all students (male and female) to succeed in math; but such efforts may be thwarted by social messages that portray math as being a difficult subject . . . particularly for females.

Social Media

Perhaps the most significant vehicle for influence today is social media. The students whom we teach are *digital natives*; they have always lived in a world in which the Internet, social media, and the ability to instantaneously communicate with others is the norm. Our students readily have access to an enormous amount of information that can both enhance and thwart their motivation.

Youth spend a great deal of time using various forms of social media. The time that youth spend using social media has increased dramatically in recent years. Whereas there certainly can be academic and social benefits derived from the use of social media, the time that students spend using social media can detract from the time that they could potentially allocate to their studies (as well as to sports, clubs, and other extracurricular activities). Although many adolescents adamantly believe that social media is a positive aspect of their lives (Rideout & Robb, 2018), research indicates that when youth use social media excessively, it can have negative effects on both academic outcomes (e.g., motivation and achievement), as well as their overall psychological well-being (LaRose, Kim, & Peng, 2011).

As teachers, we need to recognize that our students are receiving subtle and not-so-subtle messages via social media and that these messages can profoundly affect our students' motivation. In particular, **social media has the potential to perpetrate stereotypes that may influence motivation** (like the one that talking Barbie perpetrated in the 1990s). The messages that our students read and hear and see on social media can influence their values, their beliefs about what is "cool," and their long-term career aspirations. For example, results from a recent national study by Commonsense Media indicate that two-thirds of adolescents who use social media encountered "racist, sexist, homophobic, or religious-based hate content" (Rideout & Robb, 2018, p. 6).

Although we like to think that women and men have equal opportunities in today's society, there are still potent messages about gender differences that are pervasive in society and that can affect our students' motivation. Many of these messages are reinforced via social media. A recent column in the *Economic Times* pointed out that societal messages still (even today) at times discourage females from entering the STEM (science, technology, engineering, and mathematics) workforce (Tole, 2017). For example, in a recent study conducted by the Pew Research Center, a Google image search was conducted in order to collect a large sample of images on the Internet of people working in a variety of jobs. The researchers then compared the proportions of males and females depicted for each profession in the images with the true gender distributions for each profession (using data from the U.S. Bureau of Labor Statistics). The findings are displayed in Table 2.4.

As these data suggest, the images that are presented on the Internet often do not reflect the realities of the national workforce. For example, women appear in only 10% of the images of chief executives, while national data indicate that 28% of all chief executives are women; and women appear in 24% of the pictures of mechanics, whereas in reality only 2% of mechanics are female.

How might these inconsistencies affect student motivation? One could argue that there are both positive and negative aspects to these discrepancies. Perhaps the fact that women are overrepresented in pictures of physicians might encourage more women to consider a career in medicine (i.e., this increases the likelihood of being exposed to women in this profession).

Table 2.4 Gender and Images in Google Searches

The percentage of women in image search results for common jobs often differs from reality

Difference between estimated % of women in image search results and the actual % in each occupation who are women, according to BLS (selected jobs)

WOMEN **UNDERREPRESENTED** IN IMAGE SEARCH RESULTS

Job	Actual	Image search	Difference
Bill collector	71%	20%	-51
Medical records technician	92	57	-35
Bartender	57	29	-28
Probation officer	64	43	-21
General manager	34	15	-19
Chief executive	28	10	-18
Security guard	24	15	-9

WOMEN **OVERREPRESENTED** IN IMAGE SEARCH RESULTS

Job	Actual	Image search	Difference
Flight attendant	73	77	4
Physician	40	48	8
Model	78	88	10
Police	14	24	10
Computer programmer	21	24	13
Mechanic	2	24	22
Singer	38	62	24

Note: These estimates are rounded. See Methodology for more precise estimates. Source: Pew Research Center analysis of U.S. Google Image Search data; Bureau of Labor Statistics data. Image searches were conducted July 7-Sept. 13, 2018. Images returned by searches were conducted at other times may differ. "Gender and Jobs in Online Image Searches"

"Gender and Jobs in Online Image Searches." Pew Research Center, Washington, D.C. (2018, Dec. 17) https://www.pewsocialtrends.org/2018/12/17/gender-and-jobs-in-online-image-searches/

In contrast, the low proportion of depictions of women as chief executives or as general managers might deter some women from considering those professions.

What can we do with this information? As teachers, we need to acknowledge that societal messages (e.g., about gender and professions) can impact student motivation (we'll be addressing this in Chapter 4). But we need to in particular be aware that the prevalence of technology and the instantaneous availability of information may make these societal messages more salient than ever to our students.

How Do We Get All of These Parties to Work Together?

Right now, you might be feeling overwhelmed. This book is about the ways that you, as a teacher, can positively impact your students' academic motivation. But in this chapter, you were just reminded that there are many other variables (some within your control, and some not) that also affect their motivation. So, if all of these variables are also at play, can you really make a difference? The answer is YES!

One of the main reasons that teachers' efforts to motivate their students sometimes fail is because teachers may be unaware of the numerous other variables that are also contributing to student motivation; as we discussed in this chapter, some of these variables are obvious, but some are subtle and operate in the background. When we as educators are aware of and acknowledge the roles that these other forces play in affecting our students' motivation, we empower ourselves to be more effective in our efforts to support student motivation.

We will revisit these other influences repeatedly throughout the rest of the book, as we introduce additional strategies that you can use to motivate your students. Rather than seeing these other influences as a hindrance to your efforts, in this book I'll repeatedly encourage you to acknowledge them, and to consider how you can sometimes utilize these other variables to support your efforts.

Summing Up

In this chapter, you were introduced to some of the external and contextual factors that impact your students' motivation. Although you, as a teacher, have the potential to have a tremendous positive effect on your students' motivation, it's also important to acknowledge that there are other variables that also exert influence. You may not always be able to impact these other factors, but you need to acknowledge that they exist, so that you can make informed decisions to support student motivation.

After acknowledging that students' personalities and individual characteristics affect motivation and also recognizing that you, as a teacher, have an impact on student motivation, we focused on four additional external influences: parents, schools, communities/neighborhoods, and society at large. Although these are extremely important influences, there are many others that we could have discussed as well. John Hattie is an education researcher who has identified over 250 variables that have been demonstrated to influence academic achievement; most (if not all) of these variables also impact motivation (for a complete listing, see http://www.visiblelearningmetax.com/). It isn't necessary for you to commit these to memory or to feel that you can and should influence all of these variables; nevertheless, as we progress through later chapters, we'll keep these multiple influences in mind, so that we can continually acknowledge that our students' motivation is determined by a wide range of variables.

APPLYING WHAT YOU HAVE LEARNED

Select a specific lesson (or activity, or unit) that you are covering in class now, recently completed, or will be starting soon. Let's not focus on what you do to motivate your students for that lesson; instead, I'd like you to think about and write down one example of an additional potential influence (beyond what you do as a teacher) on your students' motivation (with regard to this lesson or activity), for each of these categories:

- How might students' personality characteristics affect motivation?
- How might an influence from the home (e.g., from a parent) affect motivation?
- How might a school-level variable (e.g., a school policy, or something about the climate/culture of the school) affect motivation?
- How might something about the community/neighborhood affect motivation?
- How might some larger societal messages or stereotypes affect motivation?

Now that you have written these down, how might your acknowledgment of these other potential influences on motivation affect your approach to this specific lesson? Does thinking about these other variables before you begin teaching a lesson impact your planning?

Hopefully, by acknowledging these other influences, you will be able to more effectively motivate your students. Throughout the remaining chapters, we'll be talking in depth about the strategies that you can use to enhance motivation, but we'll always keep these other influences in mind as well, because they will always be operating.

THE SECRET SAUCE

I'm going to start this chapter by asking you to jump right in and do an activity related to your own motivation. Please don't skip ahead—this exercise will help you to get the most out of the rest of the chapter.

Understanding Your Own Motivation

During our adult lives, we all have opportunities to take on various challenges. Some of these challenges may be fun and exciting; others may be scary and cause us to experience some anxiety. In Activity 3.1a, a list of challenges is provided in the left column. After you read each challenge, think about how **confident** you would feel about accepting the challenge and starting to do the challenge immediately (let's say, tomorrow). Place an X in the box that represents your level of confidence for each challenge; don't skip any and answer all of these, even if you know you would never actually consider attempting one of these challenges.

Activity 3.1a How confident are you about starting each challenge tomorrow?

Challenge	Confidence				
	Not at all confident	A little confident	Somewhat confident	Very confident	Completely confident
Enroll in a graduate-level course in neuroscience.					
Bake a chocolate cake.					
Give a speech (on any topic you want) in front of 2,000 people.					

(Continued)

Activity 3.1a (Continued)

Challenge	Confidence				
Help your next-door neighbors complete their federal tax returns.					
Play golf with Tiger Woods without being nervous.					
Change a light bulb in your kitchen.					

Now, let's repeat this exercise (see Activity 3.1b), but this time, I'd like you to think about the challenges somewhat differently. Instead of thinking about your confidence about actually *doing* each of these challenges tomorrow, think about how confident you would be about **starting to learn about how to be successful at each of these challenges tomorrow** (understanding that you are just being asked to learn about the challenge, not necessarily to ever "do" the challenge)?

Activity 3.1b How confident are you about starting to learn about each challenge tomorrow?

Challenge	Confidence for Learning How to Do This				
	Not at all confident	A little confident	Somewhat confident	Very confident	Completely confident
Learn how to be successful in a graduate-level course in neuroscience.					
Learn how to bake a chocolate cake.					
Learn how to give a speech (on any topic you want) in front of 2,000 people.					
Learn how to help your next-door neighbors complete their federal tax returns.					
Learn how to play golf with Tiger Woods without being nervous.					
Learn how to change a light bulb in your kitchen.					

Most of us have a wide range of responses for the first part of this activity (3.1a). Look at your responses and notice that there is probably some variation in your levels of confidence across these challenges. Most of us are confident about taking on some challenges but not as confident with others. For example, I'm "somewhat confident" that I could bake a chocolate cake (because I have baked in the past, although not very often); I'm "completely confident" that I could change a light bulb in my kitchen (because I do this all the time); and I'm "not at all confident" that I could play golf with Tiger Woods without feeling nervous. Was there variation in your levels of confidence across these challenges?

Now, compare your responses from the first part of the activity to your responses in the second part of the activity (3.1b). Did you check the same boxes? Is your confidence about *giving* a speech in front of 2,000 people the same as your confidence to *learn how* to give a speech in front of 2,000 people? Is your confidence about helping your neighbors with their tax returns the same as your confidence to *learn how* to help your neighbors with their returns? Although I noted that I was "somewhat confident" that I could bake a cake, I'm "completely confident" that I could *learn how* to bake a cake; and although I noted that I was "not at all confident" that I could play golf with Tiger Woods, I'm "somewhat confident" that I could learn how to play without being nervous.

For most of us, our confidence in our abilities to do something and our confidence in our abilities to learn how to do something are not quite the same. As you will see throughout this chapter, this is an important distinction with regard to motivation.

The Secret Sauce

In just about any aspect of our lives, we will be more motivated to participate in an activity (e.g., ride a bicycle) if we feel confident in our ability with regard to the activity (e.g., one's ability to ride a bicycle). Someone who has changed many light bulbs will probably be confident when asked to change a light bulb; but someone who has never given a speech in front of a large group of people probably will not be confident about walking on to a stage in front of a large crowd and giving a speech.

SELF-EFFICACY

By now you've probably figured out that the "secret sauce" is confidence. The term that researchers use to discuss our students' confidence with regard to academic tasks is **self-efficacy**. Self-efficacy is defined as "beliefs in one's capabilities to organize and execute the courses of action required to produce given attainments" (Bandura, 1997, p. 3). We're going to use the term self-efficacy throughout the rest of the chapter rather than the term "confidence." We'll be doing this because, as you'll see later in this book, there are a lot of "self" terms used by educators (e.g., self-efficacy, self-concept, self-esteem, etc.), and it's very important to distinguish these terms, because they have very different meanings. Let's look a bit more closely at what we mean by self-efficacy.

Self-Efficacy Beliefs

First, self-efficacy is a belief. This is not a minor point—self-efficacy beliefs exist in our minds (and in our students' minds), along with thousands of other beliefs. Let's look at a few beliefs that we might hold:

- (A) The belief that Democrats and Republicans will never agree on taxation.
- (B) The belief that statistics is a difficult academic subject.
- (C) The belief that the earth is flat.

Do these beliefs represent your personal beliefs? You might agree with A and B, but chances are that you don't believe C. But if the year was 1347, there is a good chance that you would agree with C.

Now stop and think for a moment: What do these three beliefs have in common? At first glance, not much. But they do in fact have something in common—all of these beliefs can (at least potentially) be changed. The belief that the earth is flat was the most widely held belief about the nature of this planet for many thousands of years. This belief was deeply entrenched throughout society. But as evidence emerged suggesting that the earth is round, beliefs about the shape of the earth eventually changed. Even a long-standing belief can change, if enough evidence emerges.

Some people might have strong, long-held beliefs that Democrats and Republicans will never agree on tax policies; but that belief also *could* change if enough evidence is presented, suggesting that agreement is possible. For example, if you had the opportunity to listen to a conversation between a moderate Democrat and a moderate Republican who actually

Figure 3.1 Case Study: Scary Statistics

Jeff is 40 years old, and has decided to return to school to pursue his doctoral degree. Jeff has never felt confident about his mathematical abilities; he struggled with math during high school, and he avoided math as much as possible when he was in college. Jeff was thrilled to be accepted into a doctoral program, but he soon learned that he had to take at least two semesters of statistics in order to earn his degree. When Jeff learned this, he became highly anxious and began to doubt his ability to complete the degree. Jeff met with his statistics instructor before the first class began and explained that he has always been scared by mathematics and that he felt equally scared about taking statistics courses. Jeff's instructor told him that "nobody ever died from taking statistics" and reassured Jeff that with the right approach, Jeff could be successful in the class. Jeff's instructor worked closely with Jeff to slowly increase Jeff's self-efficacy beliefs regarding statistics (we'll talk about some of the strategies that the instructor used later in the chapter).

Fast forward: Jeff completed the two required statistics courses, and he went on to take several other advanced courses. He actually did not complete his degree, because he was offered and accepted a job doing statistical data analysis full-time.

did agree on some compromises on taxes, that might help to change your belief that Democrats and Republicans will never agree.

What about statistics? You may or may not believe that it is a difficult academic subject. If you do believe that it is difficult, could this belief be changed? Let's look at the case study presented in Figure 3.1 to examine this more closely.

This scenario is based on a true story. It's important to note from the outset that Jeff approached his instructor early on— not all of our students will take this initiative. Nevertheless, in thinking about Jeff's situation in terms of his motivation, what's clear is that his beliefs about his ability changed; so beliefs can change! Jeff's self-efficacy for learning statistics was very low due to his past experiences with mathematics. Over time, working with his instructor, his self-efficacy beliefs improved. After a while, his self-efficacy beliefs increased to the point where Jeff was able to make a major career shift and to accept a new job that he never would have imagined earlier in his life.

Courses of Action

Returning to Bandura's definition of self-efficacy, another important part of the definition states that self-efficacy involves believing that one can "organize and execute" the "courses of action" that are required to produce a desired outcome. So, what does this mean?

Let's use the example of giving a speech in front of 2,000 people. Let's say that an individual named Sally wants to be able to deliver such a speech. According to our definition of self-efficacy, Sally would need to believe that she could organize and execute "courses of action" that would produce the desired outcome (i.e., being able to successfully deliver the speech). So, Sally needs to believe that she can be successful at giving the speech (i.e., she needs to have some confidence in herself), and she needs to be able to both "organize" and "execute" courses of action that will help her to achieve her goal.

What would that mean? In terms of organizing the appropriate courses of action, Sally would need to be confident that she could plan what she might need to do to prepare to give the speech. Some of these preparations might include the following:

- Give a practice speech in front of a small group of friends in order to assess her initial levels of anxiety.

- Buy an instructional video on how to deliver a speech.

- Watch the video and do all of the practice exercises that are suggested in the video.

- Give another practice speech in front of the same group of friends and ask for their honest feedback about her performance.

- Think about and incorporate the feedback, and then give a practice speech in front of a group of colleagues (but not close friends), and ask for their honest feedback.

In terms of "organizing," Sally would need to be able to ask friends and/or colleagues to take the time to listen to her practice speech; she would need to know how to find an effective instructional video and make various other preparations. In terms of "executing," Sally would need to believe that she will actually carry out all of those courses of action. It's one thing to make a plan; but it's another to carry out the plan. Self-efficacy involves both making the plan (i.e., organizing), and carrying out the plan (executing). And don't forget that we started with a discussion of the essential role of our *beliefs* in ourselves; Sally needs to believe that she can both organize and execute these courses of action.

At this point, you're probably wondering what you, as a teacher, can do to increase your students' self-efficacy. That's where we turn next.

Instructional Strategies for Building Students' Self-Efficacy

There are some very specific actions that you can take to increase your students' self-efficacy. I've called self-efficacy the "secret sauce" because in many ways, self-efficacy is the ingredient that is needed in order for your students to be optimally motivated in your class. Whereas we will be discussing many strategies that you can use to support your students' motivation in the following chapters, it's important to recognize that if your students don't feel that they are able to learn what you are teaching them (i.e., they have low self-efficacy), then many of the other strategies that we'll discuss in this book may not work as intended. If our students are confident that they can learn the material that we are teaching them, then we will be able to use numerous other strategies (that will be introduced later in the book) to motivate them even further.

An Important Note About Self-Efficacy

Before we proceed, there is an essential piece of information that you need to understand about self-efficacy. As we have noted, students who have high self-efficacy feel confident in their abilities to learn; however, self-efficacy beliefs are highly specific. Think about your own self-efficacy as a learner. If I asked you, *"Are you confident in your ability to learn?"*, how would you respond? If you're like most people, you probably responded "yes," but also thought, "Well it depends on what I'm learning."

This is very important... it's not very informative for our students to be able to say that they feel confident in their general abilities as learners; it's much more important for them to feel confident that they can learn a particular subject area (e.g., biology, math, or reading) (Bong, 2001). It's also important that our students feel efficacious about engaging with specific academic tasks within each subject area (e.g., being confident in one's ability to solve a math problem using fractions, to read a short story, or to write a complete sentence).

Let's look at an example to see why a **general sense of self-efficacy** as a learner isn't sufficient:

Maria is a fifth grader. Her grandfather asked her the following question: "Maria, are you a good learner in school? Are you confident that you can learn a lot at school?" Maria thinks about this, and when she thinks about all of the topics that she learns about in school, overall she does feel confident; she responds to her grandfather by saying "Yes grandpa, I am a good learner; I do feel confident." He said, "That's fantastic." Maria's mother later takes grandpa aside and says, "I heard your conversation with Maria. She is confident overall, but I have to tell you that when it comes to math, she is not at all confident. So yes, overall she is a confident learner, but math is the exception."

Think about this scenario. Does it sound realistic? It should. Most of our students, when asked, can provide an overall, holistic impression of their abilities as learners (when thinking across all of their subjects). Moreover, particularly during the elementary school years, most students do consider themselves to be good learners (Nicholls, 1990). But when we dig deeper and ask them about their confidence in specific subject areas (or at doing specific assignments), we often will learn that their confidence varies across different tasks. This is a key point about self-efficacy—*when we, as teachers are trying to support our students' motivation by building their confidence as learners, we need to keep in mind that we may need to build their confidence in different ways, depending on the subject or the task or assignment.*

Modeling

One of the most powerful strategies that we can use to build our students' self-efficacy beliefs is **modeling**. Modeling essentially means "showing" our students how to do something. When students are learning new material or working on a new academic task, they initially may have low self-efficacy. However, observing or listening to a demonstration of someone successfully engaging with the material or doing the task improves students' self-efficacy beliefs with regard to the new skill (Bandura, 2019). As teachers, we can model the mechanics of how to do something (e.g., how to draw a parallelogram), and we can also model our thought processes (e.g., how we go about solving a particular math problem). In addition, as we will discuss below, the teacher doesn't always have to be the model—other students can serve as models, too. And given the availability of technology, we also often can bring models into our classrooms through online videos or live online demonstrations (e.g, via Skype or Zoom or similar applications).

Why does modeling work? Modeling is an effective strategy for increasing students' self-efficacy for several reasons:

1. When students see someone else successfully perform a task, the students will be more likely to believe that they too can successfully perform the same task.

   Example: Jeffrey, who is 12 years old, does not know how to roller skate. However, when his friend Julia demonstrates the steps that she takes preparing to skate and then actually skates, Jeffrey feels he is more likely to be successful and decides to try to skate.

2. Observing someone else perform a task often leads to a better understanding of the skills the student might need to develop in order to successfully perform the task.

   Example: Pamela decided to sign up for a pottery class. She was somewhat intimidated about using the potters' wheel. However, after observing her instructor demonstrate the steps involved, she felt more confident and decided to give it a try. After a few attempts, Pamela successfully created a bowl.

3. When students observe how models cope with challenges while completing a task, the students learn strategies that they can utilize if they experience challenges or frustration.

   Example: Jamilah is in the eighth grade and taking Spanish I this year. For homework one evening, Jamilah has to answer five questions in complete sentences in Spanish. Although she finds this a bit challenging, Jamilah vividly remembers sitting at the kitchen table in past years, watching her older sister use an online Spanish-English dictionary for support when doing the same kinds of homework assignments. Jamilah then finds the online dictionary and is able to confidently complete the homework.

What are the characteristics of effective models? When students observe anyone modeling the steps to complete a novel task, their self-efficacy is likely to be enhanced. However, there are several characteristics of models that may increase the positive effects of observation (Bandura, 1997; Schunk, Meece, & Pintrich, 2014).

1. **Similarity**. It's more effective for students to observe models whom they perceive to be similar to themselves. Some of the characteristics of models that might be perceived as being similar include:
   - Gender
   - Age
   - Ability

This doesn't mean that the model has to be identical on all characteristics; however, if the model is similar in one or more ways, that can be helpful. Here are two examples:

- Lexie, who is 10 years old, is learning how to plant flowers. She will probably gain greater confidence observing another child planting flowers compared to observing an adult.
- Tom, who is 15 years old, is not very athletic. Tom wants to learn how to play basketball. Tom will probably benefit more from observing another 15-year-old who also is not very athletic but has learned how to shoot the basketball into the hoop reasonably well compared to observing a 17-year old who is the school's star basketball player.

2. **Competence**. Our students will pay more attention to (and take more seriously) models who are able to successfully and confidently carry out the tasks that they are demonstrating. When we prepare to demonstrate something to our students, we need to consider how prepared we (as teachers) are. As educators, we are always developing our own knowledge, and we will need to learn and demonstrate new skills for our students. Consider the following example:

- A sixth-grade language arts teacher asks his students to make presentations using PowerPoint. The teacher decides to give the class a demonstration on using PowerPoint. However, the school has recently upgraded to a new version of PowerPoint. When the teacher gives the presentation, he is clearly uncomfortable with the new version of the software, and he makes several silly mistakes.

Although well-intentioned, this demonstration will probably not be very effective. The students' confidence in their own abilities to prepare a presentation using PowerPoint may not improve much if they see their teacher struggling.

3. **Attitude**. The attitude of the presenter matters as well. A friendly, enthusiastic presenter is much more effective than a presenter who seems unfriendly or bored during the demonstration. Consider the following two descriptions of teachers demonstrating how to divide fractions:

- Mrs. Smith starts the lesson with a big smile; while going over an example, she concentrates, very aware of the tone of her voice, and she expresses enthusiasm throughout the lesson. She conveys to the students that she is actually having fun dividing fractions.

- Mrs. Hanks is not looking forward to teaching this lesson; her negative attitude is quite obvious to the students. She doesn't smile, and she speaks in a monotone voice. Moreover, she does not make eye contact with the students.

If you were learning how to divide fractions, from which teacher would you like to learn? Clearly Mrs. Smith's lesson is more appealing than Mrs. Hanks's lesson. But let's move beyond the entertainment value of the lessons and focus on self-efficacy. Research shows that Mrs. Smith's enthusiasm and positive demeanor will instill a sense of confidence in her students (Frenzel, Taxer, Schwab, & Kuhbandner, 2019). The students are more likely to pay attention to Mrs. Smith's lesson; and the learning of new material can only occur when students pay attention to the lesson!

 STRATEGY 3.1

Modeling

When preparing any lesson, consider providing a model for your students. This could include a model of how to think about something (e.g., how you think your way through a problem), or a model demonstrating how to "do" something. If you are not comfortable modeling the activity, try to find a video that can provide a model for your students.

Setting Short-Term Goals

The types of goals that we set for ourselves, or that others set for us, can affect our self-efficacy (Schunk, 1984). Let's try Activity 3.2a to see how this works. Imagine that you plan to go on a diet. Imagine that you have taken each step described in the left column; after you read each step, read the corresponding question (in the right column), and write down your answer.

Activity 3.2a Dieting

Steps		Write down your answer to each question below after reading the corresponding step.
1. Imagine that you have decided to go on a diet. You set a goal of losing twenty-five pounds within six months.	→	How confident do you feel about being able to lose twenty-five pounds in six months?
2. You decide that you will only check your weight once per week. At the end of the first week, you weigh yourself, and you have lost one pound.	→	How do you feel at the end of week one?
3. At the end of the second week, you weigh yourself again, and you have lost one additional pound.	→	How do you feel at the end of week two?
4. At the end of the third week, you weight yourself again, and you have lost one additional pound.	→	How do you feel at the end of week three?
5. After three weeks, you review you overall progress; you have lost three pounds toward your goal of losing twenty-five pounds.	→	How motivated are you to continue with the diet, given your goal of losing twenty-five pounds?

How did you feel about dieting? Did you initially feel somewhat confident, but then become less confident as time progressed? Did you still feel confident after week 1, but then lose confidence each subsequent week? Many people respond as follows:

1. How confident do you feel about being able to lose twenty-five pounds in six months? *"I'm not certain, but I'm fairly confident that I can stick with my diet and be successful."*

2. How do you feel about losing one pound after the first week? *"I feel pretty good about it, I stuck to my diet, and I lost a pound. Off to a good start."*

3. How do you feel about losing one additional pound at the end of the second week? *"Okay I guess, but I kind of thought I would have lost a bit more by now; I've been doing this for two weeks now."*

4. How do you feel about losing one additional pound at the end of the third week? *"I don't feel good about it.*

Maybe I'm not good at dieting; it's just not working for me. I'll never get to 25 pounds."

5. How motivated are you to continue with the diet, given your goal of losing 25 pounds? *"I'm not sure I want to keep going. I'm frustrated. For some reason I'm just not succeeding. It has been three weeks, and I only lost three pounds."*

Were your answers somewhat similar to these? For most of us, it is frustrating to feel as though we are not making progress (or making progress too slowly), and not achieving our goals. If the goal is to lose 25 pounds, and after three weeks, only three pounds have been lost, most people will be disappointed. Many people start their diets feeling quite confident that they can be successful (i.e., they have high self-efficacy for dieting); but if we don't make sufficient progress, we lose our confidence, and are likely to stop trying.

Now, let's stop and hit "reset." In Activity 3.2b, I present the same exercise, but I have changed it ever so slightly; notice in particular that the goal mentioned in step 1 is different this time. Take a moment to redo the exercise:

Activity 3.2b Dieting Revisited

Steps		Questions for You to Consider
1. Imagine that you have decided to on a diet. You set a goal of losing one pound per week.	→	How confident do you feel about being able to lose one pound per week?
2. You decide that you will only check your weight once per week. At the end of the first week, you weigh yourself, and you have lost one pound.	→	How do you feel at the end of week one?
3. At the end of the second week, you weigh yourself again, and you have lost one additional pound.	→	How do you feel at the end of week two?
4. At the end of the third week, you weigh yourself again, and you have lost one additional pound.	→	How do you feel at the end of week three?
5. After three weeks, you review your overall progress; your goal was to lose one pound per week, and after three weeks, you have in fact lost three pounds.	→	How motivated are you to continue with the diet, given your goal of losing one pound per week?

Compare the answers that you wrote down in Activity 3.2a to the ones you wrote down for Activity 3.2b. Did you answer the questions differently this time? What's the difference between the scenario in the two versions of the activity? The only difference is that in Activity 3.2a, the goal was to lose 25 pounds over 6 months; in 3.2b, the goal is to lose one pound per week.

Most people feel more confident at the end of each week and are more motivated to continue with their dieting when they have met their goal (i.e., losing one pound per week). In the first part of the activity, there was only a long-term ("distal") goal of losing a large amount of weight over a rather long (six-month period of time), but there were no short-term goals; in the second version of the activity, there was only a short-term ("proximal") goal of simply losing one pound per week.

Now let's do some math . . . if you were to set the short-term goal of simply losing one pound per week (as presented in 3.2b), then how many pounds would you lose in six months? If there are 52 weeks per year, then in six months you would have lost one pound per week, or about 26 pounds (even better than the 25 you had wanted to lose!). And if you were able to stick with your diet as presented in the first version of the activity (with only a long-term goal of losing 25 pounds in six months), you'd be at the same point in six months. But chances are that you might not have continued dieting with only the six-month goal; in contrast, while it's still hard work to lose one pound per week, you probably would be more likely to stick with the diet, because you would have reached your goal each week.

Here is the takeaway message: When we set short-term, reachable goals, and we experience short-term successes by achieving those short-term goals, then our self-efficacy increases, and we are motivated to move on to the next short-term goal. The small successes that we achieve as we complete short-term goals lead to an "I Can" attitude. If my goal is to lose one pound per week, and I succeed each week, I'll quite likely be motivated to stick with my diet! But if my goal is a very distant goal (i.e., to lose 25 pounds in six months), I'll quite likely become frustrated and give up.

> When we set short-term, reachable goals, and we experience successes by achieving those goals, then our self-efficacy increases, and we are motivated to move on to the next short-term goal.

ACADEMIC SHORT-TERM GOALS

Let's see how this applies to academic learning. As teachers, one of the most effective strategies that we can implement with our students is to help them to set short-term goals. Students often become frustrated with their academic work when they feel as though they are not making progress;

this is often because they are only focused on a long-term goal, and in their minds, they are not making adequate progress toward reaching that goal.

Let's look at some examples of goals that students might set for themselves at different grades in school, and ways that we, as teachers, can help them to rethink their long-term goals as short-term goals (see Table 3.1).

In each of the examples in the first column, the goal is rather broad and unwieldly. For example, a fifth grader may find it very challenging to memorize the capitals of all 50 states for a quiz. The student may not know how to go about memorizing such a large amount of information and may grow frustrated while trying to memorize all of this information. However, if the child's teacher helps the child to set shorter, more reachable goals (e.g., to just work on memorizing 10 states per night), then the task becomes more manageable. The child who has the goal of memorizing 10 states per night probably can achieve this goal each evening—but what's particularly important is that by succeeding each night, the child maintains a high level of self-efficacy (because the goal has been reached), and is therefore more motivated to continue with memorizing additional states the next evening.

Table 3.1 Long-Term Goals Reconceptualized as Short-Term Goals

Original Goal	Suggested Change to Make This a Short-Term Goal
Learn how to count by 5s up to 100. (second grade)	Learn how to count by 5s, increasing by twenty per day (i.e., first day count up to twenty, second day up to forty, etc.).
Learn how to count to 100 in Spanish. (eighth grade)	Learn how to count ten numbers per week in Spanish.
Read a three hundred-page book by the due date at the end of the month. (twelfth grade)	Read ten pages per night each night of the month.
Memorize the capitals of the fifty states for the quiz on Friday. (fifth grade)	Memorize ten capitals per night, each night starting on Saturday, and then spend Thursday night reviewing them for the quiz.
Learn how to play Tchaikovsky's "March From the Nutcracker" on the violin for a solo performance. (ninth grade)	Divide "March from the Nutcracker" into five sections and work on one section each week over a five-week period.

You might have noticed that some of the original goals mention a specific deadline (e.g., "Memorize the capitals of the 50 states for the quiz on Friday"), whereas others do not (e.g., "Learn how to count to 100 in Spanish"). When there is a specific deadline for completion of a task, it is easier to break the larger goal down into short-term goals, because each of the short-term goals can be designated for completion within a specific period of time (e.g., "memorize 10 capitals per night"). When there is no specific completion date, students may need additional assistance in deciding when and how to complete each of the short-term goals.

Often the long-term goal can only be reached if several different short-term goals are completed. Our students may need help in learning how to break a complex task down into several simpler steps. For example, Mrs. Swift, a tenth-grade Language Arts teacher, has asked the students in her class to write a five-paragraph essay discussing the character that they find the most interesting in the book, *Great Expectations* (by Charles Dickens); she assigns the essay on a Friday and tells the class that the completed essay is due in one week.

In this case, the long-term goal is to write an essay about the most interesting character in the book. Let's look at how two students approach the task:

1. Mandy doesn't start thinking about the essay until the next Tuesday. That evening, she sits down with her laptop and just starts to write. She writes a few paragraphs and then doesn't look at the essay again until Thursday. Thursday night, she reads over what she had written, and it doesn't make a lot of sense to her. She feels frustrated and tries to rewrite the first part and complete all five paragraphs; she completes the essay, but she knows that it's not very good.

2. Reese decides to break the task down into several smaller tasks as follows:
   - Saturday: He thinks about the characters in the book and decides which one to write about.
   - Sunday: He writes an outline for the essay.
   - Monday: He writes the first paragraph, introducing his favorite character.
   - Tuesday: He writes three paragraphs, each addressing a different reason explaining why the character is his favorite.
   - Wednesday: He writes a concluding paragraph.
   - Thursday: He proofreads the essay and makes final edits.
   - Friday: He turns in the essay.

Hopefully, it's obvious to you that Reese's plan is more likely to lead to success than Mandy's plan. The primary reason why Reese is likely to be successful is because rather than focusing on one overarching goal (to write the essay), Reese has broken this down into several short-term, reachable goals. As Reese achieves each of these short-term goals, he maintains his confidence in his overall ability to write the essay and is motivated to continue each day pursuing the next short-term goal until success is achieved. In contrast, Mandy has not set any shorter-term goals; consequently, she does not experience any of the small successes along the way that could help to maintain and build her confidence.

We need to recognize that our students will quite likely not know how to set short-term goals. That's where we come in! Our students will be more motivated to continue with and complete tasks if the tasks are broken down into short-term goals. And our students will benefit in particular if they receive some feedback along the way regarding their progress with each of the short-term goals (see Strategy 3.2, below). As our students experience success with these goals, they'll be motivated to continue to keep working toward the larger, longer-term goals. But we often will need to help our students to break tasks down into these shorter-term goals. Try Activity 3.3 to explore how you might help your students to break a long-term goal down into several smaller, reachable goals.

Activity 3.3 Helping Our Students to Set Reasonable Goals

1. What was the last major project or task that you assigned to your students? (If you're not currently teaching, consider asking these questions to a friend or colleague who is currently teaching).

2. Did you break the project/task down into smaller steps to help your students to use their time effectively?

3. Did your students receive any feedback along the way as they completed each step?

(Continued)

(Continued)

4. How might you approach this project/task differently the next time that you assign it?

Try applying the questions from Activity 3.3 to projects or activities that you are assigning. This exercise is particularly useful when we are reusing an activity that we have already used in previous years; it's helpful to rethink how the lesson is presented, and to perhaps consider helping our students think about short-term goals that they'll need to achieve in order to eventually complete the full activity.

 STRATEGY 3.2
Short-Term Goals

Every day, before you begin teaching, take two minutes to think about both the goals that you will provide for your students as well as the goals that they will set for themselves. If there is any way to break a task or activity down into smaller pieces (short-term goals), then suggest those goals to your students. Remember, students won't naturally know how to break a long-term goal down into smaller, reachable goals; it's perfectly fine to help them by suggesting the shorter-term goals.

MOTIVATION MYTH

Myth: *When students have very clear long-term goals (e.g., the goal of becoming a veterinarian), they'll be motivated every day to work toward those long-term goals.*

Truth: *Students are much more likely to achieve their long-term goals when they also set short-term, reachable goals along the way. As they complete short-term goals and experience success completing those goals, they maintain their motivation to achieve their long-term goals.*

Providing Appropriate Feedback

Students' self-efficacy is increased when they receive feedback that communicates to them that they are making progress on the new task that they are learning. We'll discuss feedback in much greater depth in Chapter 6; but for now, it's important to recognize that as teachers, we can enhance our students' self-efficacy if we provide them with feedback on their progress. Students become more confident about their abilities when they recognize that they are making progress; and often the only way that they'll know that they're making progress is through our feedback. As we'll see in Chapter 6, effective feedback involves more than just simple statements such as "Good job" or "Nice work"; feedback needs to be specific ("*Joey, your essay was fantastic because you really paid attention to your paragraph structure this time*").

It's particularly helpful to our students if we give them feedback as they meet their short-term goals. Remember Jeff, who was so afraid of statistics? Jeff's self-efficacy increased because he received regular constructive feedback from his statistics instructor. His instructor regularly pointed out to Jeff not only that he was doing well on class assignments, but he also pointed out *why* Jeff was doing well (e.g., because he was asking great questions, because he was coming to office hours for extra help, and because he had joined a study group). It's not easy for teachers to provide ongoing, regular feedback to our students, particularly when we have many students; but it's very important if we want to build our students' self-efficacy.

STRATEGY 3.3
Feedback

Our students can easily become frustrated with an assignment, particularly if they have no way to gauge whether or not they are approaching the assignment correctly and making progress. Consider ways in which you can provide feedback to your students as they work on assignments (not just when they complete the assignments). For example, while students are working, you can walk around the room, check in with students, and quickly look over some of their work and give them some useful, immediate feedback (and remember, even though a student may be approaching an assignment inefficiently, try to be positive, not negative in your approach).

Summing Up

In this chapter, I introduced the "secret sauce:" self-efficacy. We are going to discuss many other aspects of motivation throughout this book, but if our students do not believe that they can succeed with a particular academic task (e.g., adding fractions) or within a particular subject domain (e.g., geography), then many of the other strategies that will be presented in this book will not be very effective. Self-efficacy is necessary (not just sufficient) if we want to enhance our students' motivation.

I presented three ways that teachers can increase students' self-efficacy. These included modeling, setting short-term goals, and providing appropriate feedback. We also noted that self-efficacy is specific with regard to a lesson or activity; while a student may report generally high self-efficacy for a subject area (e.g., music), the student actually may have high self-efficacy for some activities (e.g., learning how to play the guitar), but low self-efficacy for other activities (e.g., learning how to play the flute). In addition, we noted that in some cases, it's helpful to distinguish between self-efficacy for learning something (e.g., learning the rules for how to conjugate verbs in French), and self-efficacy for doing something (e.g., actually being able to successfully conjugate verbs in French).

○ APPLYING WHAT YOU HAVE LEARNED

Some of the material that we teach is more complex and difficult to learn than other material. Select a topic (or a lesson) that is somewhat complex (i.e., a topic that students often have difficulty learning); in other words, select a topic (or lesson) for which your students are likely to at least initially have low self-efficacy.

Based on what you have learned in this chapter, how might you teach your students about this topic with the goal of increasing their self-efficacy? Prepare a lesson plan for the presentation of this topic considering the strategies that you might incorporate in order to help your students to gain confidence.

THE SECOND SECRET SAUCE

CHAPTER

4

Do you remember learning about certain topics and thinking to yourself, "Why am I learning this? When will I ever need to know this?" Moreover, if you asked your teacher why you are learning about something, or when you might use the information that you are learning about later in life, did your teacher have a good answer? I distinctly remember registering to take an art history class when I was in college; I was reluctant to take it because I wasn't very interested in art. During the first class, the professor said, "Don't ask me why people need to know about art history; it will give you something to think about in the dentist's office." That was enough for me . . . I dropped the class that day. (In retrospect, I know the professor meant well, but his comment clearly affected my motivation negatively . . . more on this later.)

In this chapter, we're going to take a closer look at what our students think about the content that we are teaching them. Specifically, we'll be examining how we present content to our students and the types of messages that we convey to our students about what we are teaching. Let's start by exploring how much you enjoyed (or did not enjoy) learning about certain topics.

Understanding Your Own Motivation

Activity 4.1 includes a list of topics that you probably learned about when you were in school. For each of these topics, I'd like you to think about two questions:

1. *Was this an interesting topic to learn about?*

2. *Was the information that you learned useful in any way (e.g., at the time or in the future)?*

For each of the questions, respond using a 1 through 5 scale as follows:

1 = Never

2 = Occasionally

3 = Sometimes

4 = Often

5 = Always

Activity 4.1 Things I Learned So Long Ago . . .

Topic	Was this an interesting topic to learn about?	Was the information that you learned useful?
Finding the length of the third side of a right triangle, when given the lengths of the other two sides		
Learning how to multiply two double-digit numbers (e.g., 45 X 81)		
Learning how to read		
Learning how to write in cursive		
Learning about the history of medieval Europe		
Learning the names for the symbols on the table of elements		
Learning how to drive a car		
Learning how to play a musical instrument		
Learning how to play basketball		
Learning how to use Microsoft Word		
Learning how to square dance		
Learning how to balance chemical equations		

Now, look at your responses for the first question (*Was this an interesting topic to learn about?*) by looking down column two. Were your responses all similar (e.g., did you respond with mostly 4s and 5s for all of the topics), or was there some variation in your responses? Now look at your responses to the next question (*Was the information that you learned useful?*) and examine the variability of those responses. Did you feel that all of these topics were equally useful, or were some topics more useful than others?

For most of us, there is quite a bit of variation in our responses to these questions. For example, we all have diverse interests; you probably had 4s and 5s representing your interest in some of the topics, and 1s and 2s for others. Similarly, you probably indicated that some of the topics were very useful, whereas others were not. Of course, some of this variation in the perceived utility of topics has to do with the larger contexts of our lives; for example, it's probably very useful for someone who works in the field of chemistry to be able to recognize the symbols from the table of elements or to be able to balance chemical equations; however, this information may not be very useful for someone who sells furniture. But for some topics, there may not be much variation; for example, most people probably responded with a 4 or a 5 regarding the usefulness of knowing how to drive a car.

Now, please take a moment to look *across* the rows, rather than down the columns. For example, for the first topic (*finding the length of the third side of a right triangle*), did your responses vary? Did you answer in a similar way for both questions? Look at your responses across the rows for the other topics as well. Did you see variation in your responses when you look across the rows? Most of us do vary in our responses, at least for some of the topics. For example, for the topic "Learning how to use Microsoft Word," I responded with a 2 for the first question (because I didn't think that it was very interesting) and with a 5 for the second question (because it's incredibly useful for me to know how to use Word). I responded with a 4 for "Learning how to play a musical instrument" (because it was interesting to learn to play the guitar), but only with a 2 for the second question (because while it was interesting to me, it wasn't very useful for me).

So what does all of this variation in our perceptions of how interesting and how useful we feel about certain topics mean? *It means that we have a wide range of beliefs about the value of the material that we learn!* In Chapter 3, we focused on **how** our students think about their abilities to do the work that we assign to them; in this chapter, we're focusing on **what** our students think about the material that we teach. As you hopefully just experienced in this exercise, there are different ways to think about academic material. Topics that we learn (and that we teach to our students) can be perceived as interesting (or boring), and they can be perceived as useful (or not useful). As you will see in the rest of this chapter, you, as a teacher, play a pivotal role in determining how your students perceive the material that you teach; you have the power and responsibility to influence your students' interests, enjoyment, and beliefs about the usefulness of what they are learning.

The Second Secret Sauce

In Chapter 3, we focused on **self-efficacy** (i.e., our students' beliefs about whether or not they can successfully engage with and complete their academic work). Self-efficacy is one of the core aspects of student motivation—if your students don't believe in themselves as learners, and don't believe that they can succeed with their class work, then their motivation will be compromised.

But there is an equally important second "secret sauce." Our students' motivation depends on their beliefs in their abilities, but *it also depends on their beliefs about the value of what they are learning*. Thus, the broad term that we will use to describe the second secret sauce is "**value**" (also referred to as **achievement values**). When we discuss students' valuing of academic content, we're not talking about values in terms of morality (e.g., family values); rather, from the perspective of motivation, students' valuing of academic content is based on three types of beliefs about the content (Eccles & Wigfield, 2002; Wigfield & Eccles, 1992):

- **Interest/Enjoyment** of the topic: Does the topic fascinate the student? Is it thought-provoking? Does the student like learning about this topic?

- **Importance** of the topic: Is the topic significant to the student, particularly in terms of how it relates to students' self-perceptions? Does learning about this topic affirm something about how the student sees himself or herself?

- **Usefulness** of the topic: Will knowledge about this topic be useful to the student either now or in the future?

You, as a teacher, can have a tremendous impact on the development of students' achievement values toward what they are learning in school. And don't underestimate the importance of these beliefs . . . students' values are incredibly powerful. When students develop positive achievement values toward specific topics during childhood and early adolescence (e.g., toward chemistry or toward music), they are more likely to take additional advanced coursework in those subjects in the future (Wang, Chow, Degol, & Eccles, 2017). For example, when students like learning math and believe that math is useful during elementary school and high school, they are more likely to major in math once in college (Musu-Gillette, Wigfield, Harring, & Eccles, 2015).

Research also clearly indicates that the values that students develop toward academic subject areas during the K–12 school years are highly predictive of their future career choices (Lauermann, Tsai, & Eccles, 2017). For example, although females are less likely to pursue careers in STEM fields than are males (National Science Foundation, 2019), one of the most important predictors of actually pursuing a STEM career for females is positive achievement values toward STEM! When female students come to value the information they are learning about in science and math courses (i.e., they enjoy learning it, and they find it to be interesting and useful), they are more likely to pursue postsecondary studies in STEM disciplines and to ultimately have careers in STEM fields (Watt et al., 2012). Consequently, as teachers, we need to do all that we can to help our students to develop positive achievement values.

MOTIVATION MYTH

Myth: *It doesn't really matter if students think that the material is useful or important; as long as they work hard, they'll be motivated to learn it.*

Truth: *Student motivation is enhanced when students value what they are learning (i.e., when they feel that what they are learning is interesting, important, and useful).*

Influences on Achievement Values

Our students are not born liking some subject areas and disliking others; these beliefs develop over time. There are many variables that influence students' achievement values. As we will see, teachers have the unique and important opportunity to influence these values—we can use instructional practices that can increase the likelihood that our students will enjoy what we are teaching them and also find the information to be important and potentially useful. But before we consider the strategies that we can use, we need to be aware of some of the *other influences* that also affect our students' achievement values.

SOCIETAL MESSAGING

Children and adolescents form beliefs about various subject areas based on messages that they hear from their families, friends, and of course from various media sources. Here are some examples of messages that our students may regularly encounter (from friends, family, the media, and numerous other sources):

- Portrayals of students being bored in school (e.g., in TV shows and movies).

- Seeing numerous examples of males (and few examples of females) in political leadership roles.

- Portrayals of scientists as "nerds" (e.g., in books, on TV, etc.).

- Portrayals of most musicians (i.e., those who are not superstars) as being poor.

- Rarely seeing or reading about examples of students who can excel in both athletics *and* the arts.

Repeated exposure to these societal messages does impact our students' beliefs about the value of these topics. If our students repeatedly see math and science portrayed as being "nerdy," and if our students believe that being "nerdy" is something to avoid, then they may develop negative achievement values toward math and science. Remember the discussion about the talking Barbie doll (in Chapter 2) that said "Math class is tough"? If large numbers of children (mostly female) play with toys like Barbie that send the message that math is a difficult subject, then that may negatively affect the development of positive achievement values toward math; why would a child, who wants to have fun and not be bored, want to spend time learning about a subject that is "tough"?

Although societal messages do influence our students' beliefs about various subject areas, don't despair; you as the teacher can do much to help your students develop positive achievement values about academic content, despite the messages that they may encounter. In the next sections, we're going to discuss specific approaches that educators can use. We'll break these down into two categories: (a) approaches focused on helping your students to enjoy and become interested in school subjects and (b) approaches focused on helping your students see the importance and usefulness of learning about various school subjects.

STRATEGY 4.1
Societal Influences

Often, we are so busy that we don't have time to think about or talk about societal messages about the topics that we are teaching. Spend some time at the start of each month thinking about any societal messages or stereotypes that your students might have about topics that you will be teaching about (you might consider doing a quick Internet search to find out about some stereotypes that you might not be aware of). Knowing about these potential social influences in advance can help you to foster positive achievement values toward the content.

Making Content Enjoyable and Interesting

When we enjoy some type of activity, we are usually motivated to continue to partake in that activity. If you think that skiing is fun, then you'll probably be motivated to go skiing whenever you can; if you think that doing crossword puzzles is fun, then you'll probably do crossword puzzles quite often. Similarly, when our students enjoy learning about a topic, they are more likely to partake in activities related to that topic. For example, when students enjoy reading and language arts, they are more likely to read for fun at home and more likely to take additional language arts-related coursework in the future (Durik, Vida, & Eccles, 2006). Similarly, if a student learns to play the piano and truly enjoys the experience, then the student is likely to continue playing the piano (even after piano lessons or a piano class has ended).

When we consider students' interest in what we are teaching, we need to acknowledge that there are two types of interest: **individual interest** and **situational interest** (Hidi, 2001). **Individual interest** refers to long-term interest that has developed over time. For example, if a student (Jeremy) has been interested in astronomy for many years, that student has developed an individual interest in the topic of astronomy. **Situational interest** is the more immediate, in-the-moment interest that is triggered by the immediate context (e.g., by instruction, by reading an interesting article, by watching a short YouTube video, etc.). An example of situational interest would be a student (Kerri) reading an article about astronomy and coming away from the experience feeling that the article was very interesting. The difference between Jeremy and Kerri is that whereas Jeremy has developed a long-standing interest in astronomy, Kerri merely became briefly interested after reading one article. Kerri's initial interest may grow into longer-term individual interest, or it may end soon after she has forgotten about the article. As a teacher, most of the strategies that you will use will focus on triggering students' situational interest; nevertheless, if our students' interest can be maintained, we can hopefully also influence their individual interest.

For any given topic, there are many strategies that teachers can use to both appeal to students' interests and to help to make the learning experience enjoyable. However, it's essential to remember that some strategies may stimulate initial interest in a topic, whereas other strategies may be more effective at encouraging continued, longer-term interest in the topic (Mitchell, 1993). Let's examine some effective approaches:

1. **Design tasks that encourage curiosity**. Students are likely to become more interested in academic content when we can stimulate their curiosity (Brophy, 2010). As we are planning lessons, it is helpful to consider ways that we can arouse curiosity in our students. Some ways to do this include:

   - Ask an intriguing question about some aspect of the topic that you are covering, while making sure that the question is framed around something that the students can relate to or care about deeply. For example, a teacher covering a unit introducing basic economics might ask the following question to invoke curiosity: "Everybody loves our local park (Franklin Park), but as you all know, the city is experiencing financial problems and is considering selling the park site to developers. How much money would the city need to raise to be able to save our park?"
   - Introduce an interesting problem that can best be solved by learning and mastering the topic that you are covering in class. For example, during a unit on astronomy, a teacher might ask, "Besides Mars, if NASA decided to build a space station on another planet, which planet would be the best choice?"
   - Use your own curiosity as a means of stimulating your students' curiosity. Our students often think that teachers are experts and that we know everything. When we show our students that we

too are learners and are curious about various topics, it can stimulate their curiosity. Think about something that you are truly curious about (that relates to a topic that you are covering in class), and share that curiosity with the class. For example, in a language arts class, a teacher might introduce a Shakespearian play that the teacher has never read, and say, "I've really grown to love Shakespeare over the years, but I've actually never read *Much Ado About Nothing*, so I'm really curious about the plot, and I can't wait to read it with you."

2. **Incorporate fantasy elements into instruction**. By presenting material that incorporates fantasy, we can increase our students' interest in the material (Lepper, 1988; Parker & Lepper, 1987). There are many ways that fantasy elements can be incorporated into instruction. Some examples include the following:

   - In a biology class, ask students to create a new animal (one that doesn't exist), based on an existing animal; the students would then need to consider the biological ramifications of the new animal and use principles of biology to support their creations (e.g., the students might create a dog that could live under water) (Brophy, 2010).
   - In a social studies class, have students create a news broadcast, in which reporters create a news segment about a specific topic (Brophy, 2010). For example, the reporters could pretend that it is the year 1812 and prepare a segment about the War of 1812; or reporters could prepare a segment in which they present a book review (based on a book that the class is reading).
   - In a language arts lesson, ask students to substitute the characters from *Harry Potter* into a short story that the class has just read and to write about how the story might have turned out differently if the inhabitants of Harry Potter's world infiltrated the other story.

In addition, many curricular materials now come with preprepared simulations (either deliverable through technology or as in-class activities) that include elements of fantasy. Take the time to carefully look through any supplemental materials that might be available from publishers.

3. **Allow students to make meaningful choices**. As you may recall from Chapter 1, I mentioned that one of the basic psychological needs that we all experience is the need for autonomy (i.e., to experience a sense

of control, and to be able to make meaningful choices and decisions). When students have the opportunity to make choices as they learn about a specific topic, their interest in the topic often increases (Schraw, Flowerday, & Lehman, 2001). For example, suppose that a teacher is covering a unit on reptiles. The topic of reptiles might be interesting for some students but not for others. However, it is possible to stimulate situational interest in the students who initially did not want to learn about reptiles by allowing them to make some choices. Some examples of ways that choice can be incorporated include:

- Allow each student to select a reptile and to then do some research on that specific reptile.
- Allow students to select from several projects that they could do about reptiles (e.g., going to the zoo and making a video about some reptiles, working with other students to make a TV commercial about reptiles, writing a report about reptiles).
- Ask students to write a short story about reptiles; allow them to choose the topic for the story and a specific reptile, while being sure to include factually correct information about the reptile.

4. **Praise students for their individual accomplishments and growth in their individual competence, not by comparing students' accomplishments with those of other students**. While your students are engaged with their academic work, provide them with feedback that is specific to their unique work. Focus on something positive for every student. Students' enjoyment of learning about a topic increases when they see that they are making individual progress (Henderlong & Lepper, 2002). Don't focus on how a student's work compares to others' work. When students know that they are not doing as well as their classmates, they are likely to feel badly and associate those negative emotions with the topic that they are learning about; and when students know that they are doing better than others, they may become focused on continuing to outperform others and become more concerned with these social comparisons than with the topic that they are learning about.

5. **Use segments from TV shows, movies, and other media sources to generate conversation about topics**. Students greatly enjoy seeing clips from popular programs or movies and discussing those in relation to course content. For example, there are many examples of amusing clips from the popular TV show *The Big*

Bang Theory that can be used to generate discussion and interest in a wide range of science and math topics.

6. **Utilize social media to increase interest and enjoyment**. Social media platforms such as Snapchat, Twitter, and YouTube have been and always will be a part of our students' lives. Our students have never lived without social media; it is part of the fabric of their society. Therefore, it's possible for us to use this aspect of our students' lives to enhance their enjoyment and interest in learning. There are many creative ways that social media can be incorporated into your teaching with the goal of enhancing students' valuing of academic content. For example, one innovative technique that can be used to bring history or literature to life for students is to utilize social media as a means of engaging students with the content. Specifically, students can be asked to imagine that historical figures or characters in a short story or novel had access to social media (Julien, Stratton, & Clayton, 2017). For example, the students might be asked to present "tweets" (using Twitter) that historical figures might have tweeted if social media had existed when they were alive (e.g., "If Abraham Lincoln had a twitter feed, what kind of message do you think he might have tweeted with regard to slavery?").

7. **When students are working in groups, interest can be enhanced when each group member is tasked with becoming an "expert" on a specific subtopic** (Hidi, Weiss, Berndorff, & Nolan, 1998; Renninger & Hidi, 2011). Often when students are asked to work on academic tasks in groups, some students do more work than others. When each member of the group is responsible for becoming an expert on something specific, all group members feel valued and are likely to enjoy the task and possibly develop further interest in the topic; this is often referred to as the "Jigsaw" technique (Slavin, 1991). For example, a group might be tasked with preparing a presentation about Mexico City. In a group of five students, each could be responsible for becoming an expert at one of the following subtopics:

   • The city's economy
   • The city's history
   • The city's population
   • The city's geographical location and climate
   • The city's tourist attractions

8. **Select reading materials that are both well organized and that use vivid imagery**. Most of us would rather read an interesting, well organized article about current events than the congressional record.

The same is true for our students. It's important that we take the time to carefully select reading materials that will stimulate and maintain our students' interest (Schraw & Lehman, 2001). When we give our students a reading assignment (e.g., to read a chapter in the textbook), it's helpful to take the time to read (or reread) the chapter and to consider whether it is clearly organized and incorporates vivid descriptions. As teachers, we sometimes take our curricular materials for granted and forget to occasionally look at those materials (e.g., readings) with a critical eye. If you read the chapter and find it boring, then chances are that your students will as well.

 STRATEGY 4.2

Making the Content Interesting and Enjoyable

Do you ever take the time to consider whether or not the content that you are teaching is going to be interesting or enjoyable for your students? Taking a few moments to consider this and to incorporate some of the approaches that we just mentioned into a lesson can make a huge difference in terms of your students' motivation. Take a few minutes while you are planning and ask yourself if there might be a way to incorporate one of the suggestions that were just discussed into a lesson (e.g., incorporating fantasy elements, allowing students to make some choices, letting students work in small groups to learn about a particular aspect of a topic in depth, etc.).

Making Content Useful and Important

Earlier in the chapter, I asked you to think about what you learned when you were in school, and whether you ever wondered, "Will I ever use this information?" I am quite sure that when you were in elementary, middle, and high school, you often wondered about the relevance of some of what you were learning in school (I certainly did). As you might imagine, your students quite likely wonder about this in your classroom.

Let's look at an example for a specific student:

While in college, Jordan was completing requirements to become certified as a secondary school teacher. He needed to complete a course in American history for his teaching certification, so he decided to take a summer course at a local college in order to pick up those credit hours. Jordan had never enjoyed studying history; even though he was about to graduate from college, he never found history to be particularly relevant or useful when he was in middle school and high school, and he avoided taking history courses at all costs during college. Although the summer course was taught in a very dry, traditional manner (i.e., many lectures and exams based on memorization of facts), there was one discussion that occurred during that summer course that forever changed how Jordan thought about history. Specifically, the class actually had a conversation with the professor about the reasons why it is important to study history. At one point during the conversation, the professor said, "One of the reasons that we study history is because we can learn from the past; sometimes we don't want history to repeat itself, and by knowing about our past, we can better chart our future." This was an "a-ha" moment for Jordan; although he had spent many years studying history in elementary and secondary school, none of his teachers had ever taken the time to actually talk about why we study history... or to consider historical events within the context of present-day events. From that day forward, Jordan had a renewed understanding regarding why it is critical to learn history. He still didn't always enjoy learning about it, but he clearly understood why it was so important.

Does this scenario sound realistic? Is it possible for someone to get through 12+ years of school and partially through college and not understand why we study history? Well I have a confession to make... Jordan is actually me! This is a true story. Although I had some great social studies teachers over the years, none of them ever took the time to truly point out that it's essential to understand history in order to understand the world we live in today; moreover, I don't recall much emphasis or discussion in middle school and high school social studies classes about how lessons that we learn from our history can inform our future. The discussion in that summer course was a pivotal time for me, and I have looked at history through new eyes from that day forward.

My experience is not unique. Many students do not enjoy learning about social studies while they are actually in school. Interestingly, although research suggests that many students perceive social studies/history as boring and not very useful (Schug, Todd, & Beery, 1982), they sometimes later start to appreciate history as adults. One social studies teacher noted that he often encounters people who say, "I hated history as a kid, but I like it now" (Milo, 2015).

When students believe that what they are learning is important (whether it's history, math, or music), they are more likely to continue to believe in the importance of the topic in the future, more likely to take additional coursework in that area, and to consider a career in that area (Durik et al., 2006; Lauermann, Tsai, & Eccles, 2017). One of the most well-researched areas is gender and math, wherein research quite clearly indicates that when female students come to believe that mathematics is a useful subject, they are more likely to value math and to aspire to careers that involve the use of mathematics (Watt et al., 2012).

There are several approaches that teachers can take to help our students appreciate that various topics that they are learning about are both important and useful. Although our students may encounter stereotyped messages about school subjects through the media and from others (e.g., "Math is tough"), there is much that we can do to counter those messages.

1. **Ask your students to write down (anonymously) their feelings regarding the usefulness of a topic you are covering in class**. Often, we may assume that our students understand the utility value of the content that we are teaching when in reality they may not. If a fourth-grade teacher is teaching a unit on how plants grow, the teacher might ask the students the following: "In a few sentences, tell me why you think it is important to know about how plants grow." The teacher may understandably assume that students will find the information valuable; after all, we all encounter plants constantly in our lives (e.g., at home, while walking our dogs, in the supermarket, etc.). However, we really shouldn't make that assumption; many of our students probably couldn't care less about plants! By asking your students to answer this simple question before you start a new unit, it will help you to assess what you might need to do in order to help your students to understand that this is in fact valuable information.

2. **Specifically point out the relationships between course content and the real world**. When we teach about a topic year after year, as teachers we usually understand why the topic is important and how knowledge of the topic can be useful in the real world. It's easy to assume that our students will automatically make these connections for themselves, but that often is not the case. We often need to remind ourselves that our students may not see the relevance of what we are

teaching, and we may need to help them to make those connections. Table 4.1 provides examples of some topics and ways that teachers could tie the class content to the real world.

Table 4.1 Relating Content to the Real World

Topic	Why is this content useful/relevant?
Learning how to use a spreadsheet	"Everyone has to pay taxes, and as you get older and hopefully earn more money, your taxes become more complicated. Using a spreadsheet can be incredibly helpful, because you can easily keep track of your expenses throughout the year and then hopefully save money at tax time."
Learning how to speak French	"Knowing a second language will help you in many ways. Believe it or not, you will meet a lot of people who speak French throughout your lifetime, and you'll want to be able to communicate with them. Knowing some French also will help you because you'll be able to travel to French-speaking countries, to establish friendships with people who speak French, to read French books and magazines, to watch French movies, and to conduct business with people in many other countries."
Learning about the branches of government	"When you turn 18, you will be eligible to vote. Sometimes we just think about major elections like voting for the president, but in fact we all have the responsibility to vote for candidates across all of the branches of government. Sometimes a single vote makes all the difference! Every vote counts, so by understanding something about the branches of government, you'll be able to make informed decisions."

3. **Regularly communicate to parents about the utility value of information being taught in school.** Remember the story that I described earlier about my experience with history? I shared this to illustrate that many adults have not learned to appreciate the utility value of some of the content that we learn in school. When teachers inform or remind parents about the practical value of material being covered in class, parents will be more likely to reinforce the utility of the content at home. This can have positive effects on students; for example, in one recent study, when parents were provided with information and reminders about the utility value of mathematics and science content, their children on average took nearly a full semester of additional math or science during high school compared to students whose parents did not receive this information (Harackiewicz, Rozek, Hulleman, & Hyde, 2012).

4. **Ask your students to write a few sentences or even a brief essay about why a topic that you are covering in class is useful.** This is different from the first suggestion where you just asked your students if they saw a topic as useful; with this one, you are not asking them if the topic is useful; you're asking them to think about and come up with one or several reasons on their own. For example, you could ask your students both to write about (a) how the topic relates to their own lives and (b) why the topic might be important for them to know about in the future (e.g., because it might be useful in a future job). Writing assignments of this nature can increase students' interest in the material and may lead to increased achievement in class (Hulleman, Kosovich, Barron, & Daniel, 2017).

STRATEGY 4.3

Is What I'm Teaching Useful?

Take some time to think about how you can convey information to your students about the usefulness of the content that you are teaching. Everything that we teach is relevant somehow, but it often isn't obvious. Again, it can be helpful to do a quick Internet search to find some examples of applications of just about any content. Just saying a few sentences about the usefulness of a topic might make all the difference in the world for some of your students.

MOTIVATION MYTH

Myth: *There is really very little that teachers can do to make class lessons interesting and enjoyable.*

Truth: *There are many strategies that teachers can use to make lessons interesting and enjoyable. Teachers should take a few moments every day to consider how interesting and enjoyable the topic might be for the students.*

Summing Up

Imagine that you are teaching a unit on geology, and at the end of the unit, you overheard one of your students saying, "I got an A on the test, but that unit was so stupid and boring . . .

when will I ever need to know about rocks? Waste of time." How would you feel after hearing this?

As teachers, we spend much of our time focusing on student achievement. Our job is to help students learn, and learning usually means acquiring knowledge and skills. But it is also important for us to help our students to increase their interest in learning, their enjoyment of learning and their beliefs in the utility of what they are learning. Recall the anecdote that I shared about the art history class that I enrolled in during college. I went into the class with serious doubts about whether I would enjoy the class or find the content useful. When the professor made a sarcastic comment about the content being useful if we have nothing to think about in a waiting room, that sealed the deal for me—no reason to take that class! If students learn what we teach them, but then never want to learn anything else about that topic, is that a desirable outcome? Obviously, there are some topics that some students will not value (not every student is going to love learning every topic); but in some situations, our students may develop a dislike for a subject area or topic prematurely and consequently rule out potential advanced studies or even careers related to that topic, like I did with the art history class.

In this chapter, I introduced the second "secret sauce": **achievement values**. As teachers, we need to support our students' learning, but we also should do all that we can to instill positive attitudes in our students about what they are learning. When students develop positive achievement values with regard to a topic or subject, a host of positive long-term outcomes can result. These are summarized in Table 4.2.

Table 4.2 Short-and Long-Term Outcomes of Achievement Values

When students enjoy learning about a topic, find the topic interesting, and believe that the topic is useful, they are more likely to . . .
. . . take advanced courses related to that topic in the future
. . . engage with the topic (or related topics) when not required to (e.g., to read more about the topic)
. . . engage with the topic more deeply (e.g., to critically think about the topic)
. . . learn more about the topic
. . . achieve at higher levels (e.g., get good grades on assessments of their learning of that topic)
. . . use more effective learning strategies
. . . consider future careers in that area
. . . eventually choose careers in that area
. . . continue to be interested in the topic in the future
. . . believe that it is worth spending time engaged with this topic

Developed using the following sources: Eccles & Wigfield, 2002; Harackiewicz et al., 2012; Lauermann, Tsai, & Eccles, 2017; Nagy, Trautwein, Baumert, Koller, & Garrett, 2006; Wigfield & Eccles, 1992.

There are many strategies that teachers can use to support the development of positive achievement values in our students. Strategies that enhance our students' enjoyment of what we are teaching, interest in our lessons, and beliefs that the information will be useful in the real world all enhance achievement values. It's essential for our students to learn information, but if they also come away from that learning with positive attitudes and feelings about the content, then we've truly succeeded.

⚲ APPLYING WHAT YOU HAVE LEARNED

As teachers, we are asked to cover a great deal of material with our students. Nevertheless, we all need to acknowledge that some topics are simply not as interesting or enjoyable to our students as are others. Hopefully, after reading this chapter, you now have some strategies that you can implement to try to remedy this situation.

Think about a topic that you regularly teach, and that your students find boring (we all have those topics in our curricula!). Before you proceed, answer the following question about that topic: **Why do you think that your students find the topic to be boring?**

Next, think about the different aspects of achievement values that we discussed in this chapter (i.e., enjoyment, interest, importance, and utility). Write a paragraph in which you reconceptualize the way that you teach about this particular topic, so that you can incorporate some strategies to enhance your students' valuing of the topic. You don't necessarily have to address all of the ideas that we discussed in this chapter (i.e., you may not be able to make every topic enjoyable and interesting and important and useful); but think about how you might incorporate at least one or two of these into your instruction.

After you complete this activity, save this paragraph in a place where you will easily find it the next time you will be planning to teach this topic!

PART II
TEACHER PRACTICES TO SPARK MOTIVATION

HOW SHOULD I TEACH?

In the last two chapters, we discussed the central roles that students' beliefs about their abilities (Chapter 3) and their beliefs about the value of the content that they are learning (Chapter 4) play in their motivation and achievement. In the next few chapters, we're going to examine an array of instructional practices that affect students' ability beliefs and valuing of academic content. Indeed, your students' learning is a function not just of *what you teach*, but also of *how you teach*. Although as teachers we aren't always able to select the curricular materials that we are required to use, we do get to make many decisions about how we will present those materials to our students. Those decisions are critical and can profoundly affect both students' current motivation as well as their longer-term motivation.

Understanding Your Own Motivation

The choices that we make regarding how we will teach our students can affect their motivation. Let's do some self-exploration to see how these choices might affect your own motivation. In Activity 5.1a, there is a list of eight different learning activities in the left-hand column, and there is a list of eight different approaches to learning in the right-hand column. There are three parts to this activity:

1. For each learning activity listed in the left column, select the approach that you ideally would like to use (from the right column) if you were learning that content; you can use any of the approaches more than once, and it's perfectly fine if you simply omit some of the approaches. Write the letter of the approach that you select on the line printed before each learning activity:

Activity 5.1a Learning Activities and Approaches

Learning Activity	Learning Approach
____ 1. Learn how to speak Japanese.	A – Learn by watching an instructional video.
____ 2. Learn how to play piquet (a French card game).	B – Learn by using an interactive software package.
____ 3. Learn how to breed goldfish.	C – Learn by listening to a lecture.
____ 4. Learn how to change the oil in your car.	D – Learn by working cooperatively in a small group of peers, all of whom are learning this concept for the first time (they're beginners like you).
____ 5. Learn how to make the perfect soufflé.	E – Learn by working cooperatively in a small group where some people are better than you at this activity, and some are worse.
____ 6. Learn how to design a website.	F – Learn by competing with others in order to win a prize for learning more quickly than anyone else.
____ 7. Learn how to fly a small airplane.	G – Learn by being given a strict time limit in which you have to master the material.
____ 8. Learn how to play the flute.	H – Learn by "doing"—immediately immersing yourself in the task and learning by just doing it.

2. Now, repeat step one, but this time you can only use each "learning approach" once; in other words, you need to match each learning activity in the left-hand column with **only one** of the eight learning approaches in the right-hand column.

3. Next, let's assume that you are the student and I am the teacher; I'm going to assign each learning activity and require you to learn it using a specific approach *that I have selected for you.* Read the list of activities and assigned approaches presented in Activity 5.1b and then write down how you would feel about having to learn using the mandated approach.

Finally, take a moment to reflect on these three steps. How did you feel in step one when you were given the opportunity to choose any approach? How did you feel in step two when you could choose how to approach the task but your choices were limited? And how did you feel in step three when you were mandated to approach the task in a very specific way?

Our students find themselves in each of these three situations from time to time. Sometimes we simply tell our students how

Activity 5.1b Mandates Approaches to Learning

Learning Activity	Mandated Learning Approach	How would you feel about learning this way?
1. Learn how to speak Japanese.	Learn Japanese by watching an instructional video.	
2. Learn how to play piquet (a French card game).	Learn how to play piquet by using an interactive software package.	
3. Learn how to breed goldfish.	Learn how to breed goldfish by listening to a lecture describing how to breed goldfish.	
4. Learn how to change the oil in your car.	Learn how to change the oil in your car by working cooperatively with a small group of peers who have about the same experience as you with automotive maintenance.	
5. Learn how to make the perfect soufflé.	Learn how to make the perfect soufflé by working cooperatively in a small group where some people have a lot of cooking experience, and others are just beginners.	
6. Learn how to design a website.	Learn by competing with others where there is a prize for the person who develops the best website.	
7. Learn how to fly a small airplane.	Learn by being given a strict time limit in which you have to master flying an airplane.	
8. Learn how to play the flute.	Learn by picking up a flute and just playing with it via trial and error.	

to approach a learning task (e.g., what you had to do in step three); sometimes we let our students choose how to approach a learning task from a limited set of options (e.g., what you had to do in step two); and sometimes we let our students have free rein and approach a task however they would like to. Each of these situations has implications for student motivation. Nevertheless, most of the time, we as teachers make these choices for our students. As you probably saw in step three, some of the choices may make sense (e.g., learning how to play piquet by using an interactive software program), whereas other choices may not be ideal (e.g., having to learn how to fly a plane in a limited period of time). In the rest of this chapter, we will explore the decisions that you make about how you will teach and how those decisions affect your students' motivation.

A Daily Question: How Do I Teach?

How often do you ask yourself this question? If you teach the same material every year, do you just pull out the lesson plans from last year and teach the material the same way that you always have? Or do you think about how you taught the lesson in the past and make changes to your instructional approaches from time to time? Do you consider how the ways that you teach affect your students' motivation?

As teachers, we all should be thinking about how we teach every day. Yes, every day! Although we may not be able to choose the curricular materials that we will use (e.g., the textbooks), we are able to choose the ways that we present the material. And the choices that we make about instruction have effects on our students' motivation. We're now going to look at some of the many decisions that teachers can make daily with regard to the question, "How do I teach?"

How Do I Present New Material to My Students?

As teachers, we are constantly presenting new material to our students. Most of us present new material every day. Sometimes this new material simply builds on the previous day's lesson; at other times, we are introducing entirely new topics or units to our students. There are many different methods that we can use to present new material. A few of these include

- giving a brief lecture on the material;
- assigning a reading about the material;
- showing a brief video about the material;
- asking students to do some research and then share what they have learned about the material; and
- giving students a question to answer or a problem to solve, so that the students will have to acquire and use the new information in order to answer the question or solve the problem.

These are just a few examples; there are of course many other ways that we can present new material to our students. Now, think about how often you vary the instructional strategies that you use with your students in Activity 5.2.

Activity 5.2 How Do I Teach?

For each of the instructional methods listed below, estimate how many times you used this method over the past month with your students by putting an X in the appropriate box.

Method	Never	Once or Twice	Three to Five Times	Five to Ten Times	Every Day
Give a brief lecture.					
Assign a reading for students to do at home.					
Assign a reading for students to do in class.					
Show a video.					
Ask students to do some research on the topic.					
Give the students a problem to solve that uses the content.					
Have the students work in a group on an assignment or a project.					
Have students complete a worksheet.					

Now, take a look at the boxes in which you marked an X. Reflect on what you see; over the course of a month, do you use all or most of these methods? Are there some that you use quite often and others that you rarely or never use?

In terms of student motivation, it's a good idea to use a variety of instructional practices to present material when we can; students generally are more deeply engaged with learning when they are exposed to a variety of effective instructional practices (Raphael, Pressley, & Mohan, 2008). Whereas it is important for our students to learn routines and to expect structure, it's equally important to introduce some novelty into our instruction—students sometimes misbehave because they become bored with repetitive, predictable daily routines. And as boredom increases, motivation to learn decreases (Tze, Daniels, & Klassen, 2016).

When it's possible, try to use a variety of diverse instructional practices when presenting new material as opposed to always presenting new information in exactly the same way.

Practicing and Perfecting

When we present new information to our students, one of the central questions that we need to consider is how and when our students will have the opportunity to practice and master the content. In terms of students' motivation, this is a very important consideration; if our students are not given enough time to master the content that we are covering in class, they may become frustrated and might even give up on trying to learn the material. Moreover, if students do not master the content that we are teaching and then we move on to new content, the students can fall behind and just give up (particularly if mastery of the previous content is essential for understanding the new content). In contrast, if our students are given too much time to master a topic, they may become bored and distracted and also might give up.

So how much time is enough time? Students do learn more effectively and are more likely to retain what they've learned when they have the opportunities to practice what they have learned; however, that practice should be spaced out and occur over time as opposed to being crammed into a short period of time (Cepeda, Vul, Rohrer, Wixted, & Pashler, 2008). Students are more likely to master the content and actually remember and apply what they have learned when they have had sufficient time to practice and deeply learn the material. And in the long term, they'll be more motivated in your class if they know that they will have sufficient time to master the material that you are teaching them.

⚙ STRATEGY 5.2

Provide students with sufficient time to practice and master the material.

Grouping Students

Are the students in your class all there because they have been placed into the class together because of something that they all have in common (e.g., they all have excelled in a certain subject area in the past)? Moreover, do you arrange students into small groups within your class for various instructional activities? The primary rationale for putting students into groups for instruction (either as an entire class or in small groups within a class) is that the makeup of the group will support student learning and lead to higher achievement. But what about motivation? The decision about whether or not to arrange students into groups and how to organize those groups is actually quite critical in terms of student motivation. Whereas some grouping practices allow for more targeted instruction, placing students into groups sometimes can have detrimental effects on motivation

Two of the most common ways of grouping students are **within-class grouping** (i.e., dividing students into smaller groups within a classroom), and **between-class grouping** (i.e., dividing students by entire classrooms, often by ability; this is also often referred to as **ability-grouping** or **tracking**). There are actually many ways to group students. Table 5.1 provides examples of grouping practices.

Table 5.1 Examples of Grouping Practices

Within-Class Grouping Practices		Between-Class Grouping Practices	
Within-Class Grouping Techniques	Example	Between-Class Grouping Techniques	Example
Ability Groups	*In Mrs. Marks's second grade classroom, her twenty-four students are divided into three reading groups (with eight students in each group) based on their reading skills.*	Homogeneous Ability Grouping	*At Western High School, students are grouped by ability for science instruction; students either take basic science, regular science, or advanced science.*
Cooperative Groups	*Mr. Guthrie asks his seventh-grade students to work in cooperative groups to do research about Brazilian culture.*	Heterogeneous Ability Grouping	*At Southern Middle School, all of the math classes are composed of students of mixed math abilities.*

(Continued)

Table 5.1 (Continued)

Interest Groups	Ms. Wagner asks her twelfth-grade language arts students to work in small groups of students with similar interests in reading and writing reviews of three novels.	Flexible Homogeneous Ability Grouping	Students at Eastern Elementary School are grouped by ability for math instruction, but the groups are re-assessed every five weeks and students are often moved from one group to another.
Random Groups	Mr. Jones often asks his students to work on projects in small groups; he assigns students randomly to groups, and he always forms new groups when students begin a new project.	Cross-Grade Subject-Specific Grouping	At Gracie Elementary School, the fifteen students in each of the fourth and fifth grades who have consistently demonstrated superior science ability are pulled out of their regular classes to learn advanced science together.

Although grouping students according to their abilities is a common practice, there actually are many different ways to form these groups. Ability groups can be stable or flexible. Stable ability grouping occurs when a teacher divides students into ability groups at the beginning of the academic year for instruction in a particular subject area, and students remain in the same groups for the entire year; flexible ability-grouping occurs when teachers divide students into ability groups for instruction and then reorganize membership in the various groups throughout the year based on students' current needs. Consequently, a teacher who formed three math ability groups (i.e., one for the higher-ability students, one for the lower-ability students, and one for the average-ability students) might place a student into the average group at the beginning of the year, but then notice that the student might need some extra support and additional time in learning some math concepts and move the student into the lower-ability group for a period of time. The student could then move back into the average-ability or higher-ability group at a later time with flexible ability-grouping.

So how is ability grouping related to motivation? Let's explore this with the activity in Activity 5.3.

Activity 5.3 Motivation and Grouping

Imagine that you have signed up for a short course in which you'll learn techniques to successfully invest money in the stock market. During the first class session, one of the instructors gives everyone a pretest that is designed to assess your present knowledge about investing, as well as your potential for learning the new investment techniques. When you return for the second class, the instructor projects a PowerPoint slide that lists the names of all of the class participants, with either the letter A, B, or C next to each name. You notice that there is a "C" by your name. One of the instructors then says:

"We're going to divide you into three smaller groups; you'll be in that group for the remaining nine class sessions. If you are in Group A, go to room 104; if you're in Group B, go to room 106; and if you are in Group C, stay in this room."

After the As and Bs leave the room, your instructor says, "Welcome to Group C. This group is designed to go through the material slowly and to provide easy examples to help you to learn these techniques really well. Group A goes a bit faster, and Group B is a group for people who have a lot of potential to really learn a lot during the class."

How do you feel about being in Group C? (write your answer below):

You probably have mixed feelings about being in Group C. This group is designed to move at a slow pace; moreover, the instructors seem to be implying (without explicitly saying so) that in their opinion, the students who were placed in your group don't have the potential to learn as much as do the students who were selected for Group A or B. If you're like most of us, you may feel one or more of the following:

- Somewhat upset that the instructors don't think you have a lot of potential.

- Relieved that you will have ample time to learn, because you know you're just a beginner at investing.

- Angry that whereas you paid the same amount of money as everyone else did for the class, you're not going to learn as much.

The way that you feel will affect your motivation throughout the rest of the class. If you were relieved because you know you'll have ample time to learn the material, then you'll

> Placing students into groups that allegedly reflect their abilities can—positively or negatively—impact their motivation.

probably be more motivated to work hard during the remaining sessions; but if you feel angry because you're not going to get exposed to as many investment techniques as others, then you may not be motivated to try very hard. And if you are upset because you think that you may not able to learn how to use these investment techniques, then you may give up altogether, and lose your confidence in investing. Moreover, even though the instructors may have the best of intentions by putting you into Group C, many of us would be likely to draw the conclusion that we were deemed to not be as "good" in some way as the other students. The takeaway point from this activity is to recognize that being placed into a group that allegedly reflects one's ability can impact (either positively or negatively) one's motivation.

Now, let's extend this and consider how grouping practices affect our students' motivation. Using Activity 5.4, write down your initial thoughts about any potential motivational implications for students being placed into each of the following whole-class groups for math instruction (if you prefer to substitute a different subject area for math feel free to do so); try to answer this for the age/grade level that you teach (as the effects might differ for young children compared to adolescents):

Activity 5.4 Motivation and Ability Grouping

What might be the effects of placing a student into a class for math instruction based on his or her ability?	
Type of Ability Grouping	**Possible Effects on Motivation**
Low-Ability Group	
Average-Ability Group	
High-Ability Group	

While grouping students by ability allows teachers to provide more targeted instruction, there are some potential problematic outcomes that must be recognized as well; many of these have implications for student motivation.

SOME PROBLEMATIC OUTCOMES OF ABILITY GROUPING

- Effects of ability grouping are positive but actually quite small; stronger effects are evident for gifted students, for within-class grouping and for cross-age subject grouping (Steenbergen-Hu, Makel, & Olszewski-Kubilius, 2016).

- Minority students and students from lower socioeconomic backgrounds are more likely to be placed in lower-ability groups (Oakes, 1999).

- Black and Latinx students who are placed in lower-ability groups for reading instruction during early childhood learn less over time than their peers who are not grouped for reading instruction (Lleras & Rangel, 2009).

- Acceleration (i.e., providing some students with the opportunity to learn at a faster pace or to take classes earlier than their same-aged peers) is related to higher achievement when accelerated students are compared to peers of the same age, but not when compared to older peers (Steenbergen-Hu et al., 2016).

- When students are placed into relatively stable ability groups over long periods of time, students' friendships often are limited to friendships with other students in those same ability groups (this is particularly true for high school students); therefore, low-ability students are likely to develop and sustain friendships with other low-ability students, whereas high-ability students are likely to develop and sustain friendships with other high-ability students (Oakes, Gamoran, & Page, 1992).

Have you ever considered the potential negative effects of ability grouping? Often as teachers we become accustomed to simply dividing our students into ability groups, either because (a) we've always done it that way, (b) we believe that it will support our students' learning, or (c) because it's just easier to teach students of the same ability. The idea that "it's just easier" to teach students of similar abilities is often the elephant in the room in conversations about ability grouping. It usually is easier to teach students when they all have similar abilities in a particular subject area. But there is an often, unspoken negative effect of ability grouping on motivation, particularly when students are repeatedly placed in low ability groups. Remember Secret Sauce #1 (self-efficacy) and Secret Sauce #2 (values)? Students who are consistently placed into low-ability classes for a particular subject (e.g., reading) are unlikely to develop confidence in their abilities (i.e., self-efficacy) and unlikely to value that subject area; and as we noted in Chapters 3 and 4 when students do not have confidence in their abilities or value the material, they are less likely to be motivated to study that subject area in the future . . . and less likely to enter into professions in those subject areas (Lauermann, Tsai, & Eccles, 2017).

There are actually some viable alternatives to grouping students by ability. Below I present several alternative strategies for grouping students; these strategies are designed to minimize negative effects on student motivation.

ALTERNATIVE GROUPING STRATEGIES TO ENHANCE INSTRUCTION AND STUDENT MOTIVATION

- Group students by interest. Rather than always grouping students by ability, groups can be formed based on students' interests. For example, for reading instruction, students could select their groups based on their interests. The students would then have reading and writing assignments framed around the theme that their group is exploring. For example, a teacher might arrange four groups with students being able to choose to be in a group that focuses on either (a) mysteries, (b) science fiction and fantasy, (c) friendships, or (d) current events. This type of grouping practice promotes autonomy, which we have repeatedly identified as an important predictor of intrinsic motivation.

- Group students by ability but allow students to select their groups. It is certainly possible to use ability groups for instruction but to allow students (and their parents) to choose their groups. Allowing students to select their groups fosters the belief that any student can learn any content if the student works hard enough; when students are simply placed into a group by the teacher, that sends a predetermined message to them about their abilities. If a student is consistently placed in the "low" math group, the student is likely to come to believe that the student simply is not good at math. In contrast, when a student can choose among math groups, this fosters the belief that anyone can learn math, provided that enough effort is put forth and support is provided.

- Consider the ramifications of the labels that are applied to ability groups. Whether or not students are grouped by ability within classrooms or between classrooms, the names for the groups matter. Whenever we give names to groups, students inevitably will be aware that the groups represent different abilities. Even in elementary school, when educators give cute names to groups such as "the bunnies," "the puppies, and "the kittens," children understand that the groups are actually arranged by ability (Weinstein, Marshall, Brattenasi, & Middlestadt, 1982).

- If ability grouping is unavoidable (i.e., due to school policy or other factors outside your control), try to provide some reasonably challenging tasks for students in low-ability groups. If ability grouping is being used in a particular subject area (e.g., perhaps school policy mandates it for math courses), then try to remember that if the lower ability students are always provided with rote assignments or easy tasks (which is often what happens), this will reinforce to those students that they probably do not have talent or potential in that subject area. When students in lower-ability groups are presented with challenging tasks and with sufficient support so that the students can experience success with these challenges, both their expectancies for success and their valuing of the subject can improve.

- Be flexible with grouping. When ability grouping is used, the potential detrimental effects of being in a low-ability group can be lessened when the students understand that group membership is flexible. Let's consider two students, Michael and Mitchell, who are transitioning into middle school and will be entering the seventh grade this fall:

Michael: Michael and his family went to middle school orientation at Regency Middle School; they were informed that students would be placed into math classes based on their math ability as determined by their sixth-grade teachers. Michael was placed in the low-ability math class in seventh grade.

Mitchell: Mitchell and his family went to middle school orientation at Brookside Middle School; they were informed that in middle school, there were three different types of math classes that students could take during the seventh grade. One class ("Math A") was designed to move through the curriculum at a standard pace; another class ("Math B") was designed to move through the curriculum at a more rapid pace, and to focus on more complex math problems; and the third class ("Math C") was designed to move at a slower pace than either of the other two classes and was for students who wanted to have extra time to master math concepts. All of the families were told that students could select either Math A, B, or C; moreover, they also were told that their math teachers would talk with the students and their parents both at midyear and at the end of the year about how they were doing and discuss whether or not the student wanted to change to a different class. The family also learned that there would be a summer math "camp" held for one week in the summer that was designed to help students who wanted to move to a more advanced class to catch up on any material that might not have been covered.

What are the implications for Michael's and Mitchell's motivation toward math? Michael was told by the powers that be that he needed to be in the low-ability math class; he is likely to assume that his teachers do not think that he is very good at learning math. He was not given the opportunity to work hard and hopefully succeed in a more advanced class. In contrast, Mitchell could choose his own destiny in math. In consultation with his parents and others (e.g., his teachers and perhaps his guidance counselor), he could make an informed decision about math; moreover, the school policy of allowing students to choose their placements emphasizes that the school believes that students can rise to the occasion and do well in any math class by affording students the option of choosing their own class. Mitchell is less likely to see himself as having a certain fixed level of ability in math, because his teachers and his school believe that any student can succeed in any level of math class.

- Labeling and careers. When students are repeatedly placed into a particular ability group within a subject area, that placement can affect long-term career trajectories. Students' beliefs about their current and potential ability in a subject area (e.g., science) are shaped by their academic experiences, which include experiences with ability grouping. If a student is repeatedly placed in a low-ability science class, the student is likely to develop low expectancies for success and poor achievement values in math; those low expectancy beliefs contribute to a lower likelihood of students choosing to pursue a career in a math-related field (Wang, Eccles, & Kenny, 2013).

It isn't always easy to plan for teaching students with diverse abilities in the same room, at the same time. But think about the potential long-term effects on a student who is given the opportunity to work hard and excel in a subject area . . . this might open up many possibilities for the future for some students. And students often enjoy being in mixed-ability classes. In a recent study of students' beliefs about ability grouping, many students reported that they enjoyed working collaboratively with peers in mixed-ability math classes. One student noted, "I think it's better because since there's different abilities, you can help some people and some other people can help you in return. So then you get extra help for like if you're in one of the lowers with loads of people who aren't very good at maths and there's only like one teacher then you can't get other students to help you" (Tereshchenko et al., 2019, p. 435).

MOTIVATION MYTH

Myth: *Student motivation is often enhanced when we group students by ability.*

Truth: *Grouping students by ability often does more harm than good to student motivation.*

Using Technology

When we think about how we are going to teach a particular unit or lesson, one of the issues that we need to consider is if and how we will incorporate some form of technology. Technology is regularly used in many aspects of instruction, and many books have been written about the myriad ways that technology can be incorporated into instruction. Some of the many ways that technology can be incorporated include the following:

- Video recordings
- Audio recordings
- Interactive multimedia
- Online video conversations (e.g., using Skype, Zoom, or other online communication platforms)
- Use of software (e.g., PowerPoint, Excel, etc.)
- Digital textbooks
- Smartboards
- Laptops and tablets
- Flipped classrooms (i.e., lessons and lectures are digitized and viewed outside of class, while class time is used for application and practice)

It's beyond the scope of this book to discuss the pros and cons of all of these different technologies. Nevertheless, once you decide to utilize technology in some manner, the same questions about motivation still apply. Remember the two secret sauces? They are still essential when we are incorporating technology into instruction. Even when we use technology, our students still need to (a) feel efficacious (confident) that they can successfully do the work (Secret Sauce #1) and (b) value the content that is being taught (Secret Sauce #2).

But there is another factor to consider as well when using technology. In addition to our students' still needing to feel able to engage with and learn *the content of the lesson*, they also need to feel confident (i.e., have high self-efficacy) that they *can actually use the technology*. Let's look at an example:

Mrs. Huston is a fifth-grade teacher. Her class is working on a science unit on plants. As part of this unit, each student is given a small pot of dirt and some seeds. After planting the seeds and watering them daily, small sprouts emerge. For the next part of the assignment, Mrs. Huston asks each student to select one of their baby plants and then to measure the height of the growing plant every day for each of the next 10 days. Each day, the students must record their data in a spreadsheet, and then at the end of the 10 days, the students have to use the spreadsheet to calculate the mean, median, and range of the height of their plants.

So far, this probably seems like a reasonable activity. Mrs. Huston's students have had a lot of experience using spreadsheets, so they feel comfortable using the technology to complete this task. But let's consider one particular student named Hannah:

Hannah just moved into the neighborhood and is new to this school. She is excited about growing her own plants, particularly because she and her grandmother spend a lot of time taking care of the plants in the garden at her grandmother's house. But she is anxious about having to enter the data into a spreadsheet and to then use the spreadsheet to make calculations. Hannah has never used a spreadsheet before, and in her previous school, students never used any kind of technology (not even calculators) when learning math or science.

Now let's return to our two secret sauces. Hannah clearly believes that she can successfully grow plants (Secret Sauce #1), and she also thinks that the unit on growing plants is going to be enjoyable (Secret Sauce #2). But Hannah also is anxious about using the spreadsheets. This is important in terms of Hannah's motivation—she has the confidence to engage with the content, but she does not have confidence to use the technology. This is a very important point for us to remember when we are deciding whether or not to incorporate technology into instruction. We always need to ask ourselves if our students will be able to easily and effectively use the technology. Technology can be a great asset and can enhance our students' learning, but this will only happen if the students feel competent at using the technology (and if we as teachers also feel confident at using and teaching with the technology) (Lemon & Garvis, 2016). If the students have to struggle with both the new content *and* with how to use the technology, then the technology may actually inhibit the learning of the content.

We also should consider the fact that many of our students will continue to learn via technology long after they graduate from high school. In particular, many of our students will take partially or fully online courses. Whereas there is much research on motivation in traditional learning contexts, there is surprisingly little research examining motivation in online learning environments. Nevertheless, the extant research clearly indicates that motivation is equally important in online environments (Xie & Ke, 2011). For example, the two "secret sauces" that we discussed earlier in this book are important considerations in online contexts as well as in traditional classrooms. Motivation and learning are enhanced in both face-to-face classes and online classes when students (a) believe that they are able to successfully learn the course content and (b) value the content.

Recall that in our discussion of instructional methods that are used to introduce new content, we noted that using a variety of practices can enhance motivation. The same may be true for the use of technology. Indeed, some research suggests that whereas technology can enhance motivation, effects may be stronger when students have the opportunity to use diverse types of technology (e.g., using both an interactive simulation and a spreadsheet) (Higgins, Huscroft-D'Angelo, & Crawford, 2019). In fact, even video games can enhance motivation. Although there is often a great deal of rhetoric about the dangers of using too many video games, video games have the potential at times to support the development of effective motivational strategies that students can potentially transfer to the academic domain (e.g., being persistent and effortful; not giving up in the face of failure; etc.) (Granic, Lobel, & Engels, 2014).

To Reward or Not to Reward?

Should you provide rewards when your students achieve certain accomplishments? Let's take a look at the case study presented in Activity 5.5a:

Activity 5.5a Jeopardy (Part I)

Mr. Farber is a ninth-grade social studies teacher. He believes that it will be fun to play some games in his classes, so he decides that every Friday, each of his classes will divide into two teams and play Jeopardy. The questions for the Jeopardy game are always based on material that Mr. Farber covered in class during the previous week. Each week, everybody on the winning team receives five bonus points for the week (those points count toward final grades). The students look forward to Fridays and really enjoy playing Jeopardy. They are engaged during the games, and he actually overheard a few of his students encouraging their classmates to study for the Friday Jeopardy game.

At the end of the first grading period, Mr. Farber was pleased with this activity, but he discovered that adding five bonus points per week was wreaking havoc with his grading system. Some of his students' grades became wildly inflated, and he realized that he needed to alter his approach. During the first week of the second grading period, Mr. Farber told his students the following: "Playing Jeopardy on Fridays was a lot of fun, so we're going to continue to do that this term. The only difference is that this term, there won't be any bonus points, we're just going to play Jeopardy to have fun."

Before we move any further into this topic, how do you think Mr. Farber's students responded to the elimination of the extra points for winning at Jeopardy? Write your answer below:

Now read Part II (Activity 5.5b):

Activity 5.5b Jeopardy (Part II)

When Mr. Farber told his first-period class about this change, he was very surprised by their reaction—his students were not happy! All of the students unanimously expressed their disappointment in not being able to earn points, and they made it very clear that they did not want to play Jeopardy anymore. Mr. Farber was truly flabbergasted; he was not expecting this. Perhaps even more surprising was the fact that when he repeated this message at the start of his other four classes later that same day, the students in every class had the same reaction. He was truly shocked by this. During one class, Mr. Farber said, "Well, if we don't play Jeopardy on Fridays, then we'll just do regular class work like we do the other four days of the week." One of his students then said, "Then we'll play your stupid game, but it won't be fun."

Why do you think that the students reacted this way? Write your answer below:

Were you surprised by the reaction that Mr. Farber's students had? Sadly, their reaction is quite typical. Mr. Farber's students became fixated on the reward that they could receive (the five bonus points), and the reward became more important to his students than the game. Whereas the students did learn from playing and did have fun (until the bonus points were no longer available), the focus became the prize and not the game itself.

This is actually a phenomenon that occurs quite regularly. Specifically, the provision of some type of external reward for engaging with an enjoyable task (e.g., playing Jeopardy) can actually decrease one's intrinsic motivation to engage with the task. Researchers refer to this as the over-justification effect (Lepper, Greene, & Nisbett, 1973). When students become focused on the reward, the reward can become more important than the actual task; in other words, receipt of the reward is perceived as more important than the content that is being learned. Let's consider another example:

> Amelia absolutely loves to read books; she reads in the evenings, over the weekends, and over the summer. She reads at least four books per month, usually more. This year, her fifth-grade teacher tells the students in Amelia's class that to encourage students to read, all of the fifth graders who complete reading one book per month will be invited to a pizza party for lunch on the last Friday of each month. Whereas this incentive system is well intentioned and motivates some students to read more, Amelia's parents have noticed that she now reads less than she used to. When asked why she is now only reading one book per month, Amelia says, "Why bother reading more than one? It's not worth it, I get my pizza for just reading one book."

Unfortunately, Amelia's story actually represents the experience that many students have when they are rewarded for doing something that they already enjoy doing.

In general, we should not use rewards very often. However, they can occasionally be useful (and not harm student motivation) if they are used judiciously. If and when you do use rewards, they can be effective (and not harm students' motivation) under the following conditions (Deci, 1992; Deci, Koestner, & Ryan, 2001; Lepper & Hodell, 1989; Reeve, 2006):

- When they are informational (e.g., when a student received a reward for having learned specific information, or for having used an effective strategy)

- When they are given to recognize effort or progress, as opposed to task completion or finishing a task within a specific time period

- When they are not dependent on competing with (and doing better than) other students (we'll explore this more in the next section of this chapter)

- When they are only used to spark initial interest in a topic

- When they are meaningful to the student

Try not to motivate students with rewards for activities that they already find enjoyable.

MOTIVATION MYTH

Myth: *Motivation is always enhanced when students are given rewards for completing their assignments.*

Truth: *Rewards that are simply given to students for completing a task do not enhance motivation; the excessive use of rewards can actually harm students' intrinsic motivation for a task or subject area.*

Table 5.2 provides recommendations for using rewards effectively, so that they do not diminish student motivation.

Table 5.2 Using Rewards Responsibly and Effectively

Ineffective	Effective	Explanation
Karen's dad gives her $5.00 *every time* she gets an "A" on a math test.	Karen's dad encourages her to study math every night, and when she gets an "A" on a particularly challenging test, he gives her $5.00 *as a surprise* in recognition of her hard work.	Giving $5.00 after every "A" makes Karen focus on getting the reward at all costs; it also can negatively impact positive attitudes toward math. Giving it once (unexpectedly) in recognition of her hard work gets Karen to focus on the benefits of studying every night.
Jordan's track coach gives out passes to get a free slice of pizza at a local restaurant to the 10 team members who run the fastest each week.	Jordan's track coach gives out passes to get a free slice of pizza to anyone on the team who improves their running time from the previous week.	Rewards that recognize self-improvement can encourage continued motivation, whereas rewards that are based on outperforming others can lead to the expectation of a reward, and can lead to negative affect and lower motivation for those who seldom or never receive the reward.

(Continued)

Table 5.2 (Continued)

Mr. Wagner has his eighth-grade language arts students read Charles Dickens's *Great Expectations* every year, and they always find it boring. He decides to give them candy after they read each chapter this year. 	Mr. Wagner has his eighth-grade language arts students read Charles Dickens's *Great Expectations* every year, and they always find it boring. He decides to give them candy after they read <u>and demonstrate that they understand</u> the first three chapters this year.	When introducing a topic or lesson that might not be interesting, it's okay to use an incentive or reward early on in order to encourage the students to become engaged with the lesson; however, if rewards are given repeatedly, then the students won't become interested in the topic—they'll just do what they have to in order to receive the reward.
Mrs. Carmichael has taught her tenth-grade biology students specific strategies for writing up a laboratory report; when students successfully apply those strategies, she rewards them with a *gold star*. 	Mrs. Carmichael has taught her tenth-grade biology students how to use specific strategies to write up laboratory reports; when students successfully apply those strategies, she rewards them with *a coupon to get a free burger* at a local fast food restaurant. 	If rewards are going to be used, they should be developmentally appropriate. A tenth grader would value a free burger more than a gold star.

To Compete or Not to Compete?

As teachers, we can either encourage or discourage competition among students. Let's look at how competition can be encouraged or discouraged in terms of the goals that our students pursue. When all of the students in a class are working on the same academic task (either independently or in groups), the students can approach these tasks with one of three goals (Johnson & Johnson, 1999).

- Individual Goals: Students understand that achieving a goal is solely based on one's own effort and is unrelated to how classmates are progressing toward the goal. Example: Susan is determined to learn how to tell time in Spanish. She studies her vocabulary and practices conversing about the time with her next-door neighbor, who is fluent in Spanish.

- Cooperative Goals: Students understand that they will only achieve the goal if they work together and cooperate. Example: The students in the high school band are determined to achieve an "outstanding" designation from the judges at the state fair; band members practice daily and encourage each other, so that everyone is playing their pieces in sync.

- Competitive Goals: Students understand that they will only achieve their goals if other students in the class do not achieve the same goals (or if they achieve the goals before their peers do). Example: Francisco's math teacher gives students an extra credit problem and announces that the student who is the first to solve the problem correctly will get a bonus of five points on the next test; Francisco is determined to be the first student to correctly solve the problem.

Which type of goal is most effective? This is a complicated question, and the answer in many ways depends on what we mean by "effective."

Whereas competition can sometimes lead to improved performance in physical activities, particularly for males (DiMenichi & Tricomi, 2015), competition doesn't always enhance motivation, particularly in academic domains. Kohn (1986, p. 83) described "the grim, determined athletes who memorize plays and practice to the point of exhaustion in order to beat an opposing team." And while we may assume that students experience competition as enjoyable (and many of them certainly do), that's not always the case. It's particularly important to acknowledge that competition may be experienced more positively by students based on their cultural backgrounds. For example, whereas in western countries competition is often lauded and valued, students from other cultures may be more comfortable working collaboratively toward the success of a group rather than competing with each other to achieve individually (Chen, Chung, & Hsiao, 2009). Results of a large study examining goals among early adolescents indicated that cooperative goals were related to higher achievement and more positive peer relationships than were either competitive or individualistic goals (Roseth, Johnson, & Johnson, 2008).

If you are going to encourage competition in your classroom, keep the following points in mind:

- If you incorporate competitive activities into instruction, *avoid using rewards* for the winners as those rewards can undermine intrinsic motivation.

- *Carefully consider the number of students involved in a competition.* Positive effects of competition are lower if the number of people competing is high (Garcia & Tor, 2009). This is actually a double-edged sword: Although some students enjoy competing and are energized by competition, these students are likely to be more successful in competitive settings when there are few other competitors. This occurs because it is easier for the students to assess their standing relative to others when there are only a few people with whom to compare oneself. However, the downside is that some students don't like to compete, and competing, even in small groups, may exacerbate anxiety about poor performance.

- *Consider whether competition will have negative effects for some students.* Competition can have negative effects on performance when competition encourages students to become anxious and worry about looking "dumb" or incompetent (Murayama & Elliot, 2012).

MOTIVATION MYTH

Myth: *Incorporating competition into classroom activities enhances motivation for all students.*

Truth: *In academic settings, competition must be used cautiously. Occasional competitive activities can be enjoyable. However, competition in the classroom induces anxiety in some students and leads other students to focus primarily on winning the competition rather than on learning.*

Teaching to Students' Preferred Learning Styles

You have probably heard that students have preferred **learning styles**. Some students tend to be visual learners (i.e., they like to see things while they're learning), some are auditory learners (i.e., they like to hear things while they're learning), and some are tactile learners (they like to touch things or do things). One of the choices that educators regularly make with regard to instruction concerns whether or not we will adjust our instruction to accommodate these learning styles. Let's start our discussion of learning styles by exploring your own preferred learning styles. Please respond to the questions in Activity 5.6:

Activity 5.6 Learning Styles Assessment

The ten statements below describe a variety of assignments that you are being asked to complete. After reading each assignment description, there are three choices regarding how you could do the assignment. Circle your personal preference for how you would like to do the assignment (A, B, or C) from the three options.

	A	B	C
Learn facts about the Korean War.	Use a website with many photos from the war.	Listen to an audio recording about the war.	Prepare a skit re-enacting an event from the war.
Learn how to use a new spreadsheet.	Watch a YouTube video that demonstrates the software.	Attend a 15-minute lecture about the software.	Learn the software by actually trying it out.
Learn how to square dance.	Watch professional square dancers give a demonstration.	Listen to a professional square dancer's pre-recorded talk called "Secrets to Becoming a Pro Square Dancer."	Try out some moves—actually participate in some square dancing.
Learn how to reduce your anxiety while taking tests.	Watch a demonstration of some techniques to reduce stress.	Listen to a first-hand account from a student describing how she reduced her test anxiety.	Participate in some role-play activities in which you get to practice using some anxiety-reduction techniques.
Demonstrate that you can solve an algebra equation.	Prepare a poster demonstrating the steps required to solve an equation.	Give a five-minute oral presentation describing the steps required to solve an equation.	Use manipulatives (e.g., a set of blocks) to demonstrate how to solve an equation.
Learn how to successfully grow marigolds.	Watch a short film about how to grow marigolds.	Have a conversation with a professional marigold grower.	Plant some marigold seeds and grow them into flowers.
Learn how to ride a motor-powered scooter.	Watch a friend who regularly rides scooters show you how to ride.	Listen to step-by-step instructions on how to ride a scooter.	Rent a scooter and give it a try.
Learn how to do a chemistry experiment.	Use a poster in the classroom that contains a lot of visual images that show you how to do the experiment.	Listen to the teacher carefully describe how to do the experiment.	After reading brief instructions on the experiment, go to the laboratory and actually try to do it.

(Continued)

Activity 5.6 (Continued)

Learn how to play the chords to a famous Bruce Springsteen song on the guitar.	Watch a video of Bruce Springsteen playing the song on the guitar.	Listen to the song and to a description of the fingerings for each of the chords.	Take a guitar and just try to mimic the chords and figure them out at your own leisure.
Study the Shakespearean play *Hamlet*.	Go to a local theater and see a performance of *Hamlet*.	Read *Hamlet*.	Audition for a local production of *Hamlet*.
TOTAL			

Next, add up the number of circles in each of the three columns (A, B, and C), and write the total for each in the bottom row.

As you might have figured out, the entries in column "A" indicate a preference for visual learning; the entries in column "B" indicate a preference for auditory learning; and the entries in column "C" indicate a preference for kinesthetic ("hands-on") learning. Now look at your totals. Did you circle more items in one column (e.g., the "visual" column) than in another column (e.g., the "tactile" column)? Or did you perhaps select choices from each of the three learning styles?

Time for a Surprise

I'm about to share some information that you may (or may not already) be aware of. Before I do, brace yourself, because this may be a shock to some readers... It doesn't matter if you are a visual, auditory, or kinesthetic learner, because learning style preferences are not related to actual learning! Despite the extraordinary popularity of learning styles within the education community, *research clearly and consistently suggests that tailoring instruction to match students' preferred learning styles does not lead to more effective learning* (e.g., De Bruyckere, Kirschner, & Hulshof, 2015; May, 2018; Rogowsky, Calhoun, & Tallal, 2015). Nevertheless, many educators believe in the power of learning styles, and rigid adherence to these beliefs may be particularly prevalent among early childhood educators (Nancekivell, Shah, & Gelman, 2019).

> It doesn't matter if you are a visual, auditory, or kinesthetic learner, because learning style preferences are not related to actual learning!

There are actually many different categories of learning styles. The most typical are the ones mentioned above (i.e., visual, auditory, or tactile), but there are other "styles" that have been identified (e.g., "Reading/Writing" learners, tactile learners, etc.). And of course, we all have preferences with regard to how we learn in some situations. Think about Activity 5.6—in some situations it makes sense to prefer to learn something in a particular way. For example, I would prefer to read *Hamlet* rather than to watch a production of *Hamlet* or audition for a role in a local production; however, someone else might prefer to watch a performance of *Hamlet*. And sometimes it's easier for us to learn a skill by trying to do something (e.g., to grow *marigolds*), rather than to read about how to do it. But these occasional (and sometimes appropriate) preferences **become problematic when we start to define ourselves by learning preferences and when educators tailor instruction to match our preferences (e.g., as a "visual learner").**

It's fine for us to acknowledge that our students have preferences with regard to how they learn, and it's fine for us to honor those preferences *at times*. But as teachers, we need to recognize that these are just preferences, and that sometimes our students will benefit from learning via a "non-preferred" learning style. Consider this example:

> Yara is in the sixth grade. This is the first year that Yara has had different teachers for different subject areas (prior to this year, she was in a classroom in which the same teacher taught all of the content areas). When Yara's parents received her mid-year report card, they noticed a comment written by Yara's science teacher: "Yara is wonderful in class. She is doing great, and she is very well behaved. But she never participates. I know she has so many great ideas, I'd love for her to share them in class." Yara's parents were a bit surprised by this comment, because Yara is usually quite chatty, both at home and at school. Her parents discussed this comment with Yara; they told her they were proud of her for working so hard and doing so well in science, but they were curious as to why Yara didn't speak much in class. Yara responded with this statement: "Well, someone came into one of my other classes, and they gave us a learning styles test; and I found out that I'm a visual learner! So that means I learn best by seeing things . . . so I don't need to talk in class!"

Sadly, this is a true story. Once Yara had the label of a "visual learner," she started to define herself that way and was not motivated to speak. This is troubling for many reasons. First, Yara (just like all students) needs to recognize that discussion is a very important part of the learning process. Second, labeling Yara as a visual learner led to Yara's interpretation of visual learning as a strength, *and then her incorrect conclusion that it was not worthwhile to learn via other modalities.* Luckily, Yara's teacher didn't really care about the results of the learning styles test; Yara had a great teacher, who acknowledged that students like Yara have preferences, but as teachers we have to make decisions about how we teach based on what we know about evidence-based practices . . . not solely based on what students prefer.

When you are making decisions about how to teach, don't fall into the learning-styles trap. It's perfectly fine to provide instruction through different modalities, and students are often more motivated when instruction is varied. Nevertheless, keep in mind that as teachers, we need to support our students' ability to learn in diverse ways (not just via their preferred learning style).

STRATEGY 5.4

Avoid the temptation of targeting instruction to match students' preferred learning styles; students experience the greatest benefits when they learn via diverse modalities.

MOTIVATION MYTH

Myth: *Teaching to students' preferred learning styles improves their achievement.*

Truth: *There is no scientific evidence indicating that adjusting instruction to match students' preferred learning styles has an effect on achievement.*

Promoting Growth Mindsets

If you are involved in the field of education, chances are that you have heard about **mindsets**. The idea of mindsets was originated by Carol Dweck at Stanford University. Dweck identified two mindsets: a **growth mindset** and a **fixed mindset**.

A growth mindset is characterized by the belief that "your basic qualities are things you can cultivate through your efforts" (Dweck, 2006, p. 7), whereas a fixed mindset is characterized by believing that "your qualities are carved in stone" (p. 6).

Do Mindsets Matter? There is a large body of research that demonstrates that mindsets are powerful beliefs that affect motivation. Results of numerous studies suggest that the belief in a growth mindset is related to adaptive academic outcomes (e.g., higher achievement, greater motivation, and effort), whereas the belief in a fixed mindset is related to maladaptive outcomes (e.g., lower achievement, poor motivation, and a decreased likelihood of seeking challenges) (e.g., Dweck, 2006; Dweck & Yeager, 2019; Yeager, Dahl, Dweck, 2018).

Recall that self-efficacy beliefs (Secret Sauce #1) reflect our perceptions of our abilities to be successful at a given task. Our mindsets can affect those beliefs. Students who have a growth mindset see new challenges that they encounter as opportunities for learning, whereas students who have a fixed mindset become concerned with how they might look to others while engaged in learning tasks and may avoid challenges altogether. Let's consider two hypothetical students, Jackie and Philip, who are both 12 years old and deciding whether they should enroll in advanced math next year. Both of them attend the same school, and both currently have "A" averages in math class. Jackie, who has a growth mindset, decides to take the advanced class, whereas Philip, who has a fixed mindset decides not to take the class. When asked to justify their decisions, this is what Jackie says:

> "I decided to take the advanced math class because I know I'll learn a lot; I'm up for the challenge."

In contrast, here is Philip's justification for why he did not take advanced math:

> "I know it will be hard, and I know I'll struggle with it. I'm just not very good at math. And all of my friends will think I'm really dumb if I take the class and then fail it or have to drop it."

Recall that Jackie and Philip both currently have "A" averages in math. Yet Jackie decides to take on the challenge of advanced math, whereas Philip declines this opportunity. Their decisions are characteristic of students who hold growth or fixed mindsets. Students who hold growth mindsets are eager to taken on challenges, whereas students who hold fixed mindsets are reluctant to do so, particularly because they are concerned with how they will look to others if they are not successful (Dweck, 2006).

Now let's relate Philip's and Jackie's decisions to their self-efficacy. Since Jackie is willing to take on the challenge and holds a growth mindset, she is likely to hold positive self-efficacy beliefs related to mathematics. She quite likely believes that she is capable of learning the advanced material, and that she is capable of doing what it takes to be successful in the class ("organizing" and "executing"). In contrast, Philip quite likely has low self-efficacy beliefs when it comes to math. He does not think he will be successful, and he probably lacks confidence in his abilities to do what it would take for him to be successful in the class.

> Although many of us think of mindsets as personality traits, they are not—they are beliefs, and beliefs can be changed. As a teacher, you can make the decision to work with your students to promote growth mindsets.

Therefore, our students' self-efficacy beliefs are related to their mindsets. If you hear one of your students repeatedly saying things like "I'll never be an 'A' student" or "I am not a good learner," chances are that the student holds a fixed mindset. The good news is that mindsets can be changed. Recall that when we discussed students' personality traits in Chapter 2, we noted that our students' personalities really don't have a large effect on their academic motivation. Although many of us might think of mindsets as personality traits, they are not—they are beliefs, and beliefs can be changed. As a teacher, you can make the decision to work with your students to promote growth mindsets. Here are some approaches that you can use:

- When students do poorly on tests, allow them to retake the test and improve their grades (but also provide them with the support that they need to learn the material that they had not mastered).

- Avoid using ability grouping. When students are placed into ability groups, this promotes a fixed mindset. If a student is assigned to the low-ability science class, the student is likely to develop a fixed-mindset toward science ("I was put into the "dumb" class because I'm obviously not good at learning science").

- Use language that indicates your belief in a growth mindset during instruction. For example, you might say things like "Everyone can learn this stuff, it's about taking it one step at a time and mastering the basic concepts before jumping into the advanced material."

- Spend some time talking about how the human brain works. Point out to your students that whenever someone learns something (e.g., new information, a new skill, etc.), new connections are made between brain cells (neurons). This occurs for everyone, all the time; everyone is capable of learning, because our brains are always changing (Bettinger, Ludvigsen, Rege, Solli, & Yeager, 2018; Sarrasin et al., 2018).

Summing Up

In this chapter, we discussed the decisions that we make daily about how we will teach. Whereas we often take the method that we will use to teach for granted and may not give much thought to it, these are actually crucial decisions that affect our students' motivation to learn. Specifically, we addressed the following questions:

- How should I present material?
- How much time should I provide to my students to practice and master the content?
- Should I arrange my students into groups? If so, what are the best practices for grouping students?
- How should I incorporate technology into my teaching?
- Should I use rewards?
- Should I encourage competition?
- Should I use instructional methods that are aligned with students' preferred learning styles?
- Should I try to promote the development of a growth mindset in my students?

We emphasized in particular that as teachers, we often fall into patterns of teaching the same content in the same way, year after year. But sometimes it is important to mix things up a bit and to be creative with our teaching and use a variety of instructional methods in order to motivate our students.

♡ APPLYING WHAT YOU HAVE LEARNED

Select a topic that you will be teaching soon (i.e., one that you will be starting within the next few weeks). You could either focus on one specific lesson/ activity or on the entire unit. Now, using Activity 5.7, answer the questions that we have been discussing, for that unit. For each question, consider (a) if/how

(Continued)

(Continued)

you currently address this question, (b) how you might rethink your response to this question to do things differently **when you teach this upcoming unit**, and (c) how both your current approach and the possible new approach might affect student motivation (both positively and negatively).

Activity 5.7 How Will I Teach?

Describe a topic that you will be teaching soon:			
Decisions: For each of the decisions about instruction listed below, answer the three questions to the right of each decision.	**How, if at all, do I address this now?**	**Could I rethink this and approach this differently in the future?**	**What are the effects of my current approach and the revised approach on my students' motivation?**
Presenting new material			
Helping my students practice and master the content			
Grouping students for instruction			
Incorporating technology			
Using rewards			
Using competition			
Aligning instruction with students' preferred learning styles			
Promoting a growth mindset			

WHAT ABOUT TESTING?

The word "test" brings about feelings of dread for many students. Testing is particularly relevant in discussions of student motivation. In the last few chapters, we have been discussing strategies to support students in developing their confidence as learners, and their valuing of academic content. But our focus has been on motivation with regard to academic subject areas and academic tasks—the focus has not been on testing. Nevertheless, tests (i.e., both tests that are given in class by teachers, as well as mandated and standardized tests) are regular parts of our education system, and we need to examine motivation within the larger context of testing that occurs in schools. In this chapter, we'll be examining some big questions with regard to both classroom-based testing and standardized testing. Some of these include the following:

- Should students be motivated to take tests or just to learn the content?

- Does "testing" have either a positive or negative effect on motivation?

- Does getting a good (or a bad) grade on a test have an effect on motivation?

Understanding Your Own Motivation

We all had to learn a great deal of information between kindergarten and high school graduation. Activity 6.1a contains a quiz, with 10 questions about facts that you most likely learned when you were in school. Read each question and write down the answer; if you don't know, then just leave the response blank. But don't look any of the answers up . . . just do the best that you can, and answer these by memory.

Activity 6.1a Quiz

Question	Answer
How long do butterflies typically live after emerging from a cocoon?	
How would you express the fraction 3/8 as a decimal?	
When did the Mexican-American War occur?	
What was the name of the pig in the book Charlotte's Web?	
Which Shakespearean play featured a character named Macduff?	
What is the capital of Kentucky?	
What is the name of the layer of the earth directly under the crust?	
In music, what is the term that describes a set of musical notes within an octave, arranged in order by pitch?	
Who was the president of the United States during World War I?	
What is the area of an isosceles triangle that is six inches long and five inches high?	
SCORE	

Now, before we score your quiz, I'd like you to retake the same quiz, but this time, take it as a multiple-choice quiz, by circling the best answer to each question:

Activity 6.1b Another Quiz

Question	A	B	C	D
How long do butterflies typically live after emerging from a cocoon?	Three days or less	A week or less	A month or less	Six months or less
How would you express the fraction 3/8 as a decimal?	2.67	0.38	0.375	Fractions can't be expressed as decimals.
When did the Mexican-American War occur?	1779–1781	1846–1848	1887–1889	1904–1906
What was the name of the pig in Charlotte's Web?	Edmund	Veruca	Stuart	Wilbur

Which Shakespearean play featured a character named Macduff?	*Hamlet*	*Macbeth*	*Julius Caesar*	*Romeo & Juliet*
What is the capital of Kentucky?	Louisville	Lexington	Frankfort	Paducah
What is the name of the layer of the earth directly under the crust?	Outer core	Inner core	Subcrust	Mantle
In music, what is the term that describes a set of musical notes within an octave, arranged in order by pitch?	A scale	A chord	A stanza	A key signature
Who was the president of the United States during World War I?	Theodore Roosevelt	Woodrow Wilson	Herbert Hoover	Calvin Coolidge
What is the area of an isosceles triangle that is six inches long and five inches high?	30	1.2	15	21
SCORE				

Now let's score your quizzes. Here are the correct answers:

Activity 6.1a and 6.1b Quiz Answers

Question	Answer
How long do butterflies typically live after emerging from a cocoon?	A month or less
How would you express the fraction 3/8 as a decimal?	0.375
When did the Mexican-American War occur?	1846–1848
What was the name of the pig in *Charlotte's Web*?	Wilbur
Which Shakespearean play featured a character named Macduff?	Macbeth
What is the capital of Kentucky?	Frankfort
What is the name of the layer of the earth directly under the crust?	Mantle
In music, what is the term that describes a set of musical notes within an octave, arranged in order by pitch?	A scale
Who was the president of the United States during World War I?	Wilson
What is the area of an isosceles triangle that is six inches long and five inches high?	15

How do you feel about your scores? Did you find these quizzes to be easy or difficult? Well, if you didn't get a perfect score, you are in good company. Whereas just about all of the questions in the quizzes represent curricula that are covered between Grades K through 12, as adults, many of us don't remember all of the information that we learned. Most of us will remember information that we regularly use of course; for example, someone who uses a lot of math as an adult probably had no problem answering the two math questions. But this leads to a "big question" about education—if as adults we don't remember a lot of the information that we were taught in school, was it worth learning it in the first place? And assuming that we were tested on most of this material, what was the point of learning all of this information for a test if we can't remember it years later?

I asked you to take two different versions of the quiz; was one version of the quiz more difficult than the other? Most likely you found the first version (which required you to directly recall the information from memory) more difficult than the second version (which required you to select your answer from several choices). It's always easier to recall information when it requires recognition as opposed to direct recall; however, students often study more diligently when they know that they will be required to recall the information and not just recognize it (Rohrer & Pashler, 2010).

You probably experienced some emotion while taking these quizzes and when you calculated your scores. You may have felt anxious, embarrassed, sad, happy, bored, intrigued, or a variety of other feelings. Your students have these same experiences when they take tests and quizzes. They experience an array of feelings; moreover, they often quite likely wonder why they are being asked to learn much of the material and why they are being tested on it. Now that you have explored a tiny bit of what you do (and don't) remember from your own schooling, how do you feel about the assessments that you give to your students? In this chapter, we'll explore some of these issues and provide some strategies to make testing a positive experience for your students.

The Purpose of Testing

Why do we give tests and quizzes to our students? Before we move forward, using Activity 6.2, write down the main reasons why you (personally) give tests or quizzes to your students.

Activity 6.2 Why do you give tests?

Why do you give tests and quizzes to your students? Write down the main reasons:

Most educators administer tests and quizzes in order to assess our students' learning. But there are other reasons as well. For example, some of the other reasons for giving tests and quizzes sometimes include the following:

- Teachers are required to give tests and quizzes.
- Teachers often give tests and quizzes because of inadequate training in other forms of assessment.
- Teachers give tests because parents expect it.
- Teachers give tests because we can use test results to determine where students should be placed for future learning (e.g., into advanced courses).
- Teachers give tests because when students are taking tests or quizzes, they are less likely to misbehave.

Assessments can provide helpful feedback to both students and educators (Fisher, 2019). Well-designed assessments given by teachers in our classrooms have the potential *to improve student learning*; but often the primary purpose of large-scale, standardized assessments is *to assess student learning* (i.e., accountability) without much consideration for how assessment results can support future learning (Guskey, 2003).

Stop for a moment and answer the two questions presented in Activity 6.3.

Activity 6.3 Questions About Testing

Imagine that you have just completed teaching a four-week unit on a particular topic (i.e., something that you regularly teach each year) and that you give your students a test, and the students do very well on the test, demonstrating to you that they did learn the material.

1. How do you feel about your students' performance on the test?

Now, imagine that you overhear a conversation among a group of students in your class, after the unit has been completed. You hear the students make the following comments about the unit:

- "Glad that unit is over. That was BORING."
- "Why did we spend four weeks learning that? If I never have to think about that stuff again, I'll be very happy."
- "I can't believe some people go on to study even more about that topic; what's wrong with them?"

2. How do you feel about the comments that you overheard?

You probably felt quite good that your students did well on the test; but you probably felt somewhat disheartened to learn that your students were bored with the lessons and don't want to learn any more about this topic. As teachers, we often succeed in supporting our students' learning, but we sometimes fail in supporting their **continuing motivation**. Continuing motivation is a neglected outcome in education (Maehr, 1976). Students display continuing motivation when after a unit is complete, they want to continue to learn more about the topic in the future. When the focus of our instruction is on testing, we may neglect considering continuing motivation as a valued outcome—we become laser focused on the test. The outcome of interest often is knowledge, and as teachers, we often feel that we have done a good job if our students demonstrate that they have acquired that knowledge (by recalling and using what we have taught them on exams). Nevertheless, we need to keep our students' motivation in mind as an equally important outcome. This often is evident in reading instruction—there is a danger that reading instruction, if always focused on testing and accuracy and speed, will not lead to the desire to read during one's free time (leisure reading) (Williams, Hedrick, & Tuschinski, 2008).

Why Does Everyone Hate Tests?

Most people associate the words "test" and "quiz" with unpleasant emotions. Think back to when you were in some of the following situations; how did you feel?

- Taking a mid-term exam
- Taking a final exam
- Taking a college or graduate school admissions test
- Taking your driving test
- Taking a comprehensive unit test

Most of us recall that at times we experienced feelings of anxiety, nervousness, and worry in these situations. Most of your current students may also experience unpleasant feelings before, during, and after testing; some of the emotions that your students experience around testing may be positive, and some may be negative. Although there is much variation, there is some evidence that students who are better prepared to take tests experience more positive (and fewer negative) emotions during testing. For example, research in math suggests that students with greater abstract reasoning ability experience positive emotions (e.g., enjoyment) during math tests, whereas students with poor reasoning ability experience negative emotions (e.g., anxiety and anger), and students with average-level reasoning ability often experience feelings of boredom (Goetz, Preckel, Pekrun, & Hall, 2007).

Students also dislike tests because the more time that teachers spend focused on testing, the less time we can devote to more enjoyable activities. Nichols and Berliner (2008) note the following:

> *Under pressure to prepare students to perform well in math and reading, teachers engage in repetitious instruction that boils down to isolated bits of information, leaving little time to engage in creative interdisciplinary activities or project-based inquiry.* (p. 15)

As we examine strategies to better align testing with positive motivation in our students, keep the following in mind:

- Students' attitudes toward tests get worse as students progress through school (into higher grades) (Wong & Paris, 2000).

- Another reason that students dislike tests is because a focus on testing takes class time away from academic tasks that allow for creativity and exploration.

- Students sometimes dislike tests when they haven't mastered the skills that they need to prepare for the test.

- Students dislike tests at times because they don't enjoy studying (they'd rather be doing something else).

- Students dislike tests because they fear the consequences of getting a bad grade.

Why Am I Giving This Test?

Whereas tests can be administered diagnostically with the goal of using the results to provide students with the support that they need to succeed, in reality tests are often given by teachers in order to compel students to study (even if the topics are of no interest to the students or of no practical value in the real world), so that students will focus in class and pay attention and stay engaged (Kohn, 2014).

Every time that you give an exam or a quiz, ask yourself, "Why am I giving this test?" If you can't come up with a good answer, consider whether or not it's necessary.

Why do you give tests and quizzes? Do you use the results of tests and quizzes to help your students learn more? Do you give them the opportunity to relearn material that they have not learned well (as evidenced by test results)? When we give quizzes and tests, we need to ask ourselves, as teachers, **why we are giving the quiz or test at that particular time**. Is it just because it's traditional to give a unit exam at the end of a unit? Or is it because we believe that pop quizzes keep students engaged (even though this may not always be true). As we continue to examine the relationships between testing and motivation, try to keep asking yourself to think about why you give tests and quizzes. Sometimes we may realize that there is no good reason to be giving a test!

Testing and Time

Consider the following scenario:

Katie is in the fourth grade. Her teacher wants to be sure that all of the students know their multiplication tables well, because the students need to be proficient with multiplication in order to successfully learn the fourth-grade math curriculum. Katie's teacher allows students to work at their own pace to demonstrate mastery of the multiplication tables (through the twelve-times table). The teacher has a chart on the wall with each student's name, and 12 columns (one for each of the times tables). Students can take timed multiplication tests, and earn a "check" in the column for each times table by answering all of the multiplication questions on the test correctly *within three minutes*. Katie has always been good at math, but the timed tests are making her very nervous; her anxiety is actually so high that it is affecting her ability to concentrate, and she is not completing the tests within the allocated three minutes. She asks her teacher if she can have a bit more time, but the teacher will not permit this. Katie became very sad and embarrassed because most of her classmates have successfully completed all of the quizzes, yet she still has several to complete. Whenever anyone looks up at the chart, they can see that Katie is not progressing as quickly as most of her classmates.

Sadly, this is a true story. Although Katie started the fourth grade liking math, by the end of the year, she did not like math at all. The requirement for her to be able to recall multiplication facts within a limited period of time led Katie lose to confidence in her ability to do math (Secret Sauce #1) and to start to dislike math (Secret Sauce #2).

The question here is whether or not the three-minute time limit was really necessary. Some would argue that it is important for students to be able to quickly recall basic facts, and therefore, the three-minute time limit is justified; but others would argue that the three-minute limit is artificial (i.e., why three minutes, as opposed to four minutes or two minutes?), and that the long-term costs (i.e., losing one's confidence and decreased valuing of math) outweigh the benefits of being able to quickly respond to these questions. In addition, do you remember the quiz that you took at the beginning of this chapter when you were asked to try to remember facts that you had learned in school? You probably were not able to recall all of them instantly! If you had been required to initially learn those facts and recall them in a limited period of time for a test or quiz back when you were in school, do you think you'd remember those facts any better now?

Katie's situation reminds us that we need to consider a number of issues related to **time** when we are administering assessments. Time limits on mathematics assessments (as well as other assessments) can lead to anxiety (Boaler, 2014). Some of the other questions educators should consider with regard to time include the following:

- Should I give both short quizzes during a unit *and* a unit test at the end of the unit?
- Should I give short quizzes *instead of a unit test*?
- Should I give surprise ("pop") quizzes?
- How much time should I allow for the quiz or test? Should there be time limits? If a student needs extra time to complete an assessment, is that acceptable?
- If a student can't finish a quiz or test during the class period, should the student be permitted to come back during a free period or after school to complete the test?

There are no easy answers to these questions, and research results are mixed. For example, quizzes can certainly be effective and support learning, but "pop" quizzes can induce anxiety and hinder learning. More generally, whereas some research has been conducted examining the amount of time that should be allocated for each item on a multiple-choice test, there is actually little empirical research on this topic (Brothen, 2012).

There is actually another way to think about the timing of assessments. Specifically, when we consider the reasons why we are administering an assessment, it is helpful to distinguish between formative and summative assessments. **Formative assessments** are assessments that occur regularly during instruction; they are designed to help teachers to make effective decisions about instruction and to alter instruction as needed. Formative assessments are not "tests;" they are just informal assessments of students' in-the-moment learning (D'Agostino, Rodgers, & Karpinski, 2020). **Summative assessments** generally are higher stakes assessments, designed to assess knowledge or content mastery at the end of a unit of study. With regard to timing, formative assessments occur during instruction, often quite informally, whereas summative assessments are more formal, and are administered after a unit has been completed. Characteristics of formative and summative assessments are summarized in Table 6.1.

Table 6.1 Characteristics of Formative and Summative Assessments

Formative Assessments	Summative Assessments
• Administered either before or during instruction	• Administered after instruction has ended
• Can be oral or written	• Purpose is to assess whether students have mastered the content
• Can be administered to individuals or groups	• Often used to make decisions about future course or group placement
• Usually evaluated by teachers, but can be evaluated by peers	• Often count heavily toward final grade
• Aligned with the curriculum	• No inherent assumption that additional instruction on the topic will occur
• Used to make decisions about instruction	
• Can be administered at set times or as needed	
• Criterion-referenced scoring (i.e., performance on assessment based on having learned specific content)	
• Many digital technologies are available for administering formative assessments	
• Results should be meaningful and easy to interpret for teachers and students	

Developed using the following sources: D'Agostino et al. (2020); Mandinach & Lash (2016); Shavelson et al. (2008).

What Are the Consequences of the Test?

As teachers we spend a great deal of time preparing our students for tests and quizzes, but what happens after the test is over? Have you ever thought about how your students feel after they take a test and receive the results? Does the way that a student feels after a test affect the student's subsequent motivation? One of the consequences of testing is that students' test scores sometimes have a powerful effect on their motivation. For example, one fourth-grader stated that "I know I'm good at science because I always get an A, every nine weeks, but I'm not so good at anything else" (Barksdale & Triplett, 2010, p. 10).

Let's explore this. In Activity 6.4, the left column contains descriptions of some examples of students receiving results from tests. The right column contains a list of adjectives that describe some feelings that the students might have after receiving these results. Circle all of the adjectives from the lists provided for each example that could describe how this student might feel.

Activity 6.4 Grades and Emotions

Read each situation and then circle all of the adjectives that describe how the student might feel.	
Situation	**Circle all of the words that might describe how this student feels.**
Jeff worked very hard studying for his spelling test. He just found out that he got an "A" on the test.	Happy, Sad, Angry, Confused, Disappointed, Proud, Excited, Apathetic, Satisfied, Frustrated, Emotional
Isabella usually does not get good grades on math tests. She worked really hard this time and thought that she did well, but when she got the test back, she found out that she got a "D."	Happy, Sad, Angry, Confused, Disappointed, Proud, Excited, Apathetic, Satisfied, Frustrated, Emotional
Autumn got a "B" on her latest science test, just like she always does.	Happy, Sad, Angry, Confused, Disappointed, Proud, Excited, Apathetic, Satisfied, Frustrated, Emotional
Killian thought he was doing okay in his art class, but he just found out that he got a "C" on his report card this term.	Happy, Sad, Angry, Confused, Disappointed, Proud, Excited, Apathetic, Satisfied, Frustrated, Emotional
Devin thought he wrote a really good essay for his language arts class. He was surprised to see that he got a "C" on the essay, although he did notice that his teacher gave him a lot of feedback and said he could rewrite the essay and resubmit it to improve his grade.	Happy, Sad, Angry, Confused, Disappointed, Proud, Excited, Apathetic, Satisfied, Frustrated, Emotional

(Continued)

Jordan works very hard in school and always gets good grades. Yesterday his Spanish teacher decided to give the class a pop quiz on some vocabulary words. Jordan was not expecting the quiz, and he actually wasn't prepared for it and failed the quiz.	Happy, Sad, Angry, Confused, Disappointed, Proud, Excited, Apathetic, Satisfied, Frustrated, Emotional
Jasmine often gets low grades on her social studies tests. This week, she spent a lot of time studying. Instead of her usual "C," she got a "B" this time.	Happy, Sad, Angry, Confused, Disappointed, Proud, Excited, Apathetic, Satisfied, Frustrated, Emotional

Now that you have taken some time to think about this with the examples above, have you ever realized how many different kinds of emotional responses that your students might experience after they receive assessment results from you? Let's explore this by looking at the last example (Jasmine) in greater depth. After Jasmine spent a lot of time studying and then finds out that she earned a "B" instead of a "C," she might be feeling any of the following:

- She might feel happy because her grade went up from her usual "C."

- She might feel confused or frustrated because she thought she worked hard enough to get an "A."

- She might feel angry or disappointed because her grade only went up a bit.

- She might feel proud that her grade went up to a "B."

Jasmine might be feeling any number of these ways. Nevertheless, some additional feedback from her social studies teacher could be very powerful right now and help her to process the grade. For example, Jasmine's social studies teacher might have written a note on the test that said "Great job Jasmine, I can tell that you must have really worked hard; I'm proud of you for increasing your grade, way to go!" A note of this nature might help Jasmine to experience some of the more positive emotions (e.g., she might feel proud), and consequently Jasmine, hopefully, would be encouraged to try hard again in the future. However, Jasmine's teacher also could have provided no comments; if this had occurred, without any direction, Jasmine might experience unpleasant emotions and feel sad or angry; and her subsequent motivation to study for this subject might be harmed. We'll be discussing the importance of feedback later in the chapter.

How Much Do I Talk About Tests?

As best you can, think back to last week and estimate how many times you talked about tests, quizzes, or any other graded work with your students. Prior to right now, *have you ever thought about how much time you spend talking about assessments*? Does it matter if you talk about assessments often?

By now you probably realize that this was a loaded question; of course, talking about tests matters! Think about how often you heard some of the following statements when you were a student (either in K–12 settings or in postsecondary contexts):

- "Big test coming up next week."
- "Don't forget about the quiz on Friday."
- "You never know when you might get a pop quiz."
- "You're in high school now, tests matter a lot."
- "If you don't do well on this test, it will hurt your grade for the quarter."
- "Most of you did really well on the quiz, I was quite pleased."

Let's take a closer look at the last statement in the list. Statements like this (i.e., saying that "most of you" did really well) imply that a few students did not do well (i.e., because the teacher said "most of you"); how might the students who did not do well feel when they hear a comment like this? Statements of this nature are well intentioned, but when such statements inadvertently point out to students that they did not do well when most others did succeed on the test, the students may become angry, frustrated, or embarrassed, and ultimately less motivated.

When one considers both traditional teacher-administered classroom assessments and standardized tests (which will be discussed below), it is clear that teachers often spend a great deal of class time both giving and talking about assessment-related activities. Results from a recent national survey indicated that 52 percent of the teachers who responded to the survey felt that they had to spend too much class time focused on testing (Walker, 2014).

TALKING ABOUT ASSESSMENTS DEFINES STUDENTS' ACADEMIC GOALS

The emphasis that we place on testing helps to define students' goals in a class or school. I often ask teachers to pose the following questions to their students:

What is your most important goal in this class?

If you posed that question to your students, how would they respond? Many of us expect our students to respond with a goal related to learning the content being taught. For example, in a science class, we might expect students to say "to learn as much as I can about chemistry." However, many teachers are surprised to find that their students report that their most important goal is "to get a good grade" or "to do well on the tests." If you are comfortable doing so, you might want to have an informal conversation with some of your students and ask them to respond to this question!

We actually create climates in our classrooms that are perceived by students as focusing on learning and mastery (often referred to as a **mastery goal structure**) as well as climates that focus on testing and performance (often referred to as a **performance goal structure**). The amount of time that you spend talking about testing and assessment affects the type of climate (goal structure) that your students perceive. If you talk a lot about tests and really stress the importance of tests and grades all the time, your students are likely to perceive a performance goal structure in your class; however, if you spend most of the time focusing on the actual content that you are teaching and if you support your students in mastering that content, your students are likely to perceive a mastery goal structure. It is also possible to both emphasize mastery and performance; students can perceive both mastery and performance goal structures simultaneously.

The goal structure is largely determined by the instructional practices that you as the classroom teacher use with your students (Anderman & Maehr, 1994). Some of these practices are displayed in Table 6.2.

Table 6.2 Practices That Promote Mastery or Performance Goal Structures

Practices That Promote a Mastery Goal Structure	Practices That Promote a Performance Goal Structure
Allowing students to retake tests to demonstrate mastery of a lesson or a concept	Giving a test at the end of a unit and emphasizing that the test will have a major impact on the students' grades

Allowing students to take tests when they feel that they are ready to take them (as opposed to on a specific day)	Mandating that all students take a test on the same day and at the same time
Using **criterion-referenced assessments** (i.e., an assessment in which any student can get an "A" on the test if the student demonstrates mastery of all of the topics)	Using **norm-referenced assessments** (i.e., students' test scores depend on how well other students do on the test)
Making sure that students' test results are given to them privately	Making students' test scores public (e.g., by handing tests back so that students have the opportunity to see each other's scores or by posting the scores where everyone can see them)
Providing no information to students regarding the distribution of scores in the class	Sharing the distribution of test scores with the class (e.g., "Five of you got As, and twelve of you failed.")
Spending a lot of class time focusing on the academic content, particularly emphasizing why the content that you are covering is important, and providing support so that all students can successfully learn the material	Spending a lot of class time talking about tests (e.g., "Don't forget, you have a big test on Friday.")

When teachers use instructional practices with regard to assessments that promote a mastery goal structure, students tend to adopt personal mastery goals (i.e., each student's primary goal is to truly learn and master the content), whereas when teachers use instructional practices that create a performance goal structure, students tend to adopt performance goals (i.e., each student's goal is to get a good grade, to appear competent, or to avoid appearing "dumb") (Bardach, Oczlon, Pietschnig, & Lüftenegger, 2019). And when students adopt mastery goals, they are more likely to continue to be positively motivated in the future (Anderman & Wolters, 2006).

MOTIVATION MYTH

Myth: *Intrinsic motivation is enhanced when teachers remind students daily about the importance of upcoming tests or quizzes.*

Truth: *When teachers repeatedly talk about tests and quizzes, students become focused on grades and may actually lose interest in the topic being studied.*

What About Those High-Stakes Tests?

Standardized testing is a regular part of classroom life for most students and teachers, particularly in public schools. Nevertheless, excessive standardized testing can lead to unintended motivation-related consequences, including bored students, poor teacher-student relationships, and restricting the curriculum only to material that will be covered on the tests (Nichols & Berliner, 2008). Moreover, the results of some of these standardized tests are high-stakes, because schools' scores on such tests are often reported to the public, and the scores have implications for future funding and leadership of the school. Results from a recent study of teachers in the U.S. conducted by the National Education Association indicated that 72 percent of teachers felt either moderate or extreme pressure from administrators to improve students' standardized test scores (Walker, 2014).

DEVELOPMENTAL DIFFERENCES IN ATTITUDES TOWARD STANDARDIZED TESTS

During elementary school, students often don't distinguish between regular classroom tests and standardized tests. Their attitudes toward both types of the tests are similar and often are positive. Elementary school students tend to want to do well on tests, and they try to apply appropriate test-taking strategies (Roth, Paris, & Turner, 2000). Nevertheless, even young students report some negative experiences around testing. In one study, researchers asked over 200 elementary school students from five different schools on the day after a high-stakes test to draw a picture about their experience taking the test. The drawings were then analyzed, with results demonstrating that the children reported feeling nervous, anxious, worried, isolated, and angry (Triplett & Barksdale, 2005).

By the time that students reach high school, they do distinguish between regular classroom tests and standardized tests. Moreover, they often have negative attitudes toward standardized tests (Wong & Paris, 2000). High school students also tend to employ inefficient test-taking strategies (e.g., taking short cuts or limiting their effort) during standardized tests more than do elementary school students (Roth et al., 2000). In addition, older students often are more skeptical about the value of standardized tests than are younger students (Paris, Roth, & Turner, 2000).

EFFECT OF HIGH-STAKES TESTING ON INSTRUCTIONAL TIME AND MOTIVATION

High-stakes testing does affect class time. The time spent preparing students for standardized tests has forced many teachers to sacrifice the types of lessons that are perhaps the most engaging and that promote the development of positive achievement values (Walker, 2014). Note the following descriptions of how this happens in one classroom:

> For the first six weeks of every school year, Tege Eric Lewis puts away his math books to prepare students for Indiana's statewide tests. Mr. Lewis says that for those six weeks, "we absolutely teach to the test." (Olson, 2001)

High-stakes tests can have negative effects on both student and teacher motivation. Scores on high-stakes tests can lead to either sanctions or rewards for schools. While he was president, Barack Obama stated that "Too often what we have been doing is using these tests to punish students, or in some cases, punish schools" (Kain, 2011). Research suggests that exam results more often lead to sanctions than to rewards, particularly in high-poverty schools. In addition, high-stakes tests can actually depress student interest in a subject and can be detrimental to both teacher morale and teachers' use of innovative instructional practices (Ryan & Weinstein, 2009). Finally, low achieving students who are preoccupied with not looking "dumb" may experience exceptional anxiety and consequently perform particularly poorly on high-stakes exams (Simzar, Martinez, Rutherford, Domina, & Conley, 2015).

Cheating and Testing

Have you ever caught a student cheating on a quiz, test, or an assignment? If you teach young children, you may not have encountered much cheating (or at least not any calculated, deliberate cheating); however, if you teach middle school or high school students, you quite likely have encountered cheating. Some of my colleagues and I interviewed high school students and asked them some questions about cheating. Some of the questions and answers are presented in Table 6.3.

Table 6.3 Students' Thoughts About Cheating

Question	Response
Are there particular reasons why students cheat in school?	"Um, I think there's a lot of pressure to get a good grade because as you know, um, college, a lot of students need or want scholarships and even to get accepted in the first place I think there's a lot of pressure that our society gives."
	"A lot of people know they can get away with it, so a lot of kids do it."
	"They don't want to fail. Or to do better on tests."
Is there a particular kind of student that cheats at this school?	"Actually it's kind of more often the smart kids; they're in like too many advanced classes to handle. So maybe they like… one of the easier classes they'll just copy from someone else so they can focus more on the harder courses."
	"People don't realize that the smart kids do it. The kids who aren't smart do it, and kids in the middle do it."
Do your teachers talk about cheating?	"Right before tests they say if I catch you cheating, you're out and you get an F. But people don't listen."
	"They just say 'No cheating.'"
Is there anything about a teacher that affects your decision to cheat?	"Yeah, I think if you have a teacher who genuinely seems to care about you and you have a good relationship with um I think you are less likely motivated to cheat because that would ultimately really disappoint them and hurt the relationship."
	"Well, I mean if, if they're really trying to help you understand the actual ideas then uh the work is would be easier so um you just – you just wouldn't feel the need you know it's too hard so you have to get it from someone else."
Why did you cheat?	"Really just that I needed to uh get the points for it cause, I mean right now everything's so focused around grades and getting into a good college that like you can't afford missing anything that you can avoid."
	"There's actually been a lot of instances like on tests and things like that I have. If you don't want to get a bad grade I pretty much do what I have to do not to get a bad grade. But most of the time I'm prepared for the tests so I don't have to cheat too much. but. um I actually had a project today, a trifold, had to cheat on that to get that done."

Note: Questions varied across interviews and are paraphrased in these examples; student quotes are exact quotes from students.

These responses are actually quite typical. Students cheat for a variety of reasons. From a motivation perspective, most of these reasons are related to extrinsic motivation (i.e., motivation to attain a reward like a good grade or to avoid something unpleasant, like getting punished for getting a bad grade).

Cheating is not inevitable. Research indicates that when teachers use instructional practices that create a mastery goal structure, students are less likely to cheat (Anderman, 2007). Think about this for a moment—if a teacher stresses mastery of content (rather than just learning content to take a test), there really isn't much reason to cheat. Students don't gain anything by cheating when the most important outcome is mastery of the content. Instructional practices related to cheating are summarized in Table 6.4.

Table 6.4 Instructional Practices and Cheating

Practices That Prevent Cheating	Practices That Encourage Cheating
Allowing students to take the time that they need to master content.	Having strict deadlines requiring that students must master content by a specific date.
Providing students with opportunities to correct their mistakes on tests and quizzes.	Students are not able to correct mistakes on tests or quizzes.
De-emphasizing the importance of tests and quizzes (i.e., not talking about them too much).	Constantly talking about tests and quizzes.
Criterion-referenced assessments (i.e., any student can get an "A" on a test if the student demonstrates mastery of the content).	Normative assessments (i.e., a student's grade on a test depends on how other students perform on the test).
Teaching students to use effective cognitive strategies and problem-solving skills that are aligned with the content.	Not spending any time teaching students how to use effective strategies and problem-solving skills.

Developed using the following sources: Anderman, 2007; Cizek, 1999; Murdock & Anderman, 2006.

MOTIVATION MYTH

Myth: *Teachers can't do much to prevent students from cheating.*

Truth: *Students cheat when they have a reason to cheat, and that reason is almost always to get a good grade or to avoid a negative outcome (e.g., being grounded). When teachers design instruction so that students can have the time that they need to truly master the content, students are unlikely to cheat. Remind students through your instructional practices that what's most important is what they learn . . . not what their test score is.*

Providing Feedback

When you return tests, quizzes, or assignments to your students, do you provide feedback? If you do, what kind of feedback do you provide? Moreover, do you know if your students actually pay attention to your feedback and apply it in the future?

The feedback that a student receives is one of the most critical determinants of students' future motivation. Let's engage in a thought experiment to explore this further. Read the scenario described in Activity 6.5a.

Activity 6.5a Taking a Challenging Course

Imagine that you are back in college, and you are considering enrolling in a course that is known to be very challenging. You really want to take the course, but you aren't quite sure how you will do. In the end, you decide to take the course, knowing that it will require a lot of effort.

During the first few weeks, you do feel that the course is quite challenging, but you work diligently and study every night. The first exam occurs at the end of week four. You spend a lot of time preparing for the exam. When you finish the exam, you aren't quite sure how well you did on it; you know that you answered some questions correctly, but you aren't sure about others.

Three days later....

When you return to class, the professor projects the following in front of the classroom:

10 A's

15 B's

26 C's

6 D's

1 F

The professor then hands back the exams, and you look down at yours, and you see an "F."

Describe how you feel about getting this grade:

Now, let's replay this scenario with a different ending (see Activity 6.5b).

I have asked college students to do this exercise many times; most of the time, when I ask students to describe how they feel in the first scenario (when there is no feedback provided by the professor and when the student knows that the student

Activity 6.5b Taking a Challenging Course, Part II

The scenario is the same as the one above; however, on the day when the professor returns the exam, the following occurs:

When you return to class after having taken the exam, you enter the room and you sit down at your desk. The professor then hands back the exams (**the professor does not put the distribution of test scores up for everyone to see**), and you look down at yours, and you see an "F." There also is a note written on the top of your exam that says the following:

"Don't be disheartened by this grade; I can see that you made some very common errors that a lot of students make early on in this course; I really think I can help you out with this. Please come to my office hours Wednesday morning, and we can go over this together."

Describe how you feel:

received the lowest grade in the class), almost inevitably students report that they feel "dumb," "upset," and that they "will immediately drop the course." When I ask students "to describe how they feel in the second condition (after receiving the professor's encouraging feedback and **not** knowing how their scores compared to others' scores), the students still report that they feel upset, but they seldom say that they will "drop the course," and they usually report feeling at least somewhat encouraged that they can still be successful in the course; the professor's encouraging feedback had a positive effect. Thus, *the type of feedback that a student receives on an assignment can have critically important effects on their motivation!*

Indeed, this is one of the most important tidbits of information in this entire book: your students form beliefs about what they can (and can't) do successfully, and these beliefs can shape life decisions (i.e., a student might conclude that the student is not good at learning about a specific subject and might not pursue further study or a career that might involve that subject); but your feedback can help guide them in this process. Therefore, a student who has difficulty in a biology class and receives little feedback or encouragement might entirely rule out a potential career in a biology-related field (e.g., medicine). Similarly, a student who gets low grades on language arts writing assignments and receives little feedback or encouragement might give up on the idea of a career in journalism.

> Your students form beliefs about what they can (and can't) do successfully, and these beliefs can shape life decisions!

To support your students' motivation, it is critical that you spend time providing your students with effective feedback. Feedback is effective when it directs students back toward the aspects of the content or the task that they still need to master (Kluger & DeNisi, 1996); feedback is not effective when students merely receive generic comments such as "Good job" or "Try Harder." Strategies for providing effective feedback are described in Table 6.5.

Table 6.5 Effective and Ineffective Delivery of Feedback

Effective	Ineffective
Provide feedback regularly, even if some is given informally through brief conversations.	Provide feedback only after a major exam.
Provide feedback in a manner that demonstrates that you care about the students' learning.	Provide feedback generically with little interpersonal communication.
Feedback should clearly indicate the correct answer, and why it is correct.	Feedback merely indicates if an answer is "right" or "wrong."
Feedback should be provided after students have had the opportunity to respond to the questions.	Feedback given before students have enough time to respond to the questions.
Feedback should be specific.	Feedback is very general ("Good job").
Feedback should focus on the task.	Feedback is focused on a characteristic of the student ("Don't worry—some people just aren't very good at math").
Feedback should be non-comparative.	Feedback compares the students' responses to other students' responses.
Feedback should describe next steps.	Feedback does not provide any information about how to remediate.

Developed using the following sources: Bangert-Drowns, Kulik, C.C., & Kulik, J.A. ., 1991; Koenka & Anderman, 2019; Pat El, Tillema, & van Koppen, 2012

 **STRATEGY 6.2**

Provide students with feedback that is both encouraging and realistic to help them make sense of grades on tests or assignments.

Testing and Motivation Don't Have to Be Like Oil and Vinegar

We have spent most of this chapter discussing problems associated with assessment, and how assessments negatively impact motivation. But we have to be realistic . . . assessment is not going away; we can't simply refuse to assess student learning. As educators, we will always have to assess our students' learning. In terms of student motivation, what is essential is that when we give assessments, we help our students to process feedback about their performance. When students can learn to treat mistakes that they make on assessments as opportunities for learning (rather than as indicators of incompetence), assessments can lead to enhanced motivation.

Although giving traditional tests and quizzes is often the default method that we use to assess students, there are numerous other ways of assessing learning. Some of these other assessment methods do not induce the anxiety that traditional exams often provoke. Moreover, when designing an assessment, keep in mind that although students often can effectively memorize information and recall that information on tests, they often will forget that information soon after the test if it is not regularly called upon; therefore, you might want to consider an alternate form of assessment. Here are examples of a few alternative assessment strategies that you might consider.

PORTFOLIOS

Broadly, a portfolio is a collection of student work that demonstrates a progression in learning over time. Students select exemplars of their work (referred to as **artifacts**), often along with reflections about the work. Portfolios can be presented in a variety of formats, including on paper (e.g., a showcase of written works), electronically (e.g., digitized versions of written works, often referred to as "e-portfolios"), or as a series of completed projects. E-portfolios in particular can be effective when teachers incorporate the e-portfolios directly into regular classroom practice (as opposed to treating the e-portfolios as a supplemental activity), and when teachers are trained (via coursework or professional development) in how to effectively use the portfolios to help their students self-reflect and set future goals (Beckers, Dolmans, & Van Merriënboer, 2016).

The use of portfolios supports the development of positive motivational beliefs for several reasons. First, when implemented effectively, portfolios are designed to encourage students to reflect on their learning. The portfolio provides an opportunity for students to demonstrate growth in their self-efficacy for a particular topic area; each new entry in the portfolio demonstrates the students' growing confidence in their knowledge and abilities. Second, when using portfolios, students generally are encouraged to revise their artifacts (i.e., work toward mastery), so that the portfolio truly represents a demonstration of improvement over time. Third, the artifacts that students include in portfolios often are real-world examples of applications of classroom content; the focus on realistic products of this nature can foster the development of positive achievement values toward the topic being studied (Beckers et al., 2016; McMillan, 2011; Paulson & Meyer, 1991).

PRESENTATIONS AND PERFORMANCE ASSESSMENTS

Rather than taking a traditional test, students can make presentations (either alone or in groups) to the entire class or to a smaller group of students to demonstrate mastery of content. One particularly useful strategy is to ask students to "teach" the content to others in the class as part of the presentation; when students are asked to teach the material, they have to demonstrate that they have mastered the content, and from a motivation perspective, students often enjoy activities of this nature. The students can be provided with a rubric that clearly outlines the information that must be included in the presentation. Although some students may experience anxiety in presenting what they have learned in front of others, the anxiety may be less in many cases than the anxiety that would be induced by traditional tests or exams. Moreover, in order to make an effective presentation or to teach others about a topic, students need to have a deep understanding of the material. Students do not necessarily have to think as deeply about the content when preparing for sit-down exams or quizzes.

A **performance assessment** is a type of presentation in which students actually demonstrate that they have acquired knowledge or skills. Did you ever take a driving test, or did you ever participate in a music or dance recital? Those are performance assessments. Performance assessments can be particularly useful and enhance motivation when they are used to allow students to demonstrate a newly learned skill (DiMartino & Castaneda, 2007).

Summing Up

In this chapter, we discussed the relationships between assessment and motivation. Testing is part of education, and it is not going to go away. Nevertheless, the words "test" or "quiz" don't have to induce anxiety in our students. If one of your primary goals as a teacher is to develop positive motivational beliefs in your students, and if you want your students to continue to be interested in the topic that you are teaching well into the future, then it behooves you to approach the assessment of your students' learning with this in mind.

When students feel confident that they have mastered the content that is being assessed, they tend to experience success on assessments of that content. Your students' self-efficacy is a strong predictor of performance on both low and high stakes assessments (Simzar et al., 2015). When we as teachers focus on enhancing our students' understanding of the topics that we are teaching, and when we use strategies that enhance our students' self-efficacy (see Chapter 3), our students will do better on assessments and feel little anxiety when they are being assessed.

The next time you are giving a quiz or a test to your students, try using the questions provided in Table 6.6 to engage in some self-reflection about the assessment and to consider making

Table 6.6 Self-Reflection Questions About Testing and Assessment

Question	Example
Will I provide useful feedback for the students after the assessment?	Mrs. Jeffries provides her students with feedback on their math tests, specifically indicating the types of errors that they committed. Students then have the opportunity to correct the errors and turn the corrected tests in to receive half-credit.
Does my assessment emphasize mastery or performance?	Mr. Lucas's math students take their unit tests when both he and each student agree that the student is ready to take the test.
Have I spent too much time talking about the test? Is my teaching focused on making sure the students do well on a test, or is it focused on the actual content?	Mr. Munson realized that he spends a lot of time in his seventh-grade American history class going over timelines, dates, and names, because that is the type of information that he generally asks on his tests. This week, he decided to change things, and instead of focusing on memorization of facts, he asked his students to prepare and perform skits reenacting some of the events that they have been learning about; the students must use appropriate historical information in the skits. Mr. Munson uses the skits to assess what the students have learned (instead of a traditional test).
Do I need to give this test?	Mrs. Saglio gives a grammar quiz every Friday. However, she has noticed that her students are still making grammatical mistakes that they had been quizzed on several months ago. This week, instead of a quiz, she asks her students to write a one-page review of their favorite TV shows; in their reviews, the students are required to demonstrate correct use of the grammatical concepts that they had learned that week.
Have I checked in with my students while I'm teaching a unit to make sure they are understanding the content?	Ms. Benson's students did not do well on their last Spanish test. She realized that she had not checked in with them before the test to assess how well they were learning the current material. She therefore decided to incorporate some formative assessments during the next unit, so that she could check their comprehension every other day. The formative assessments did not count toward the students' grades; they simply provided Ms. Benson with information about how well her students were learning that week's content.

some adaptations to your assessment plans so that your students see the assessment as an opportunity for growth, rather than as a measure of their competence.

This exercise is going to require you to think out of the box . . . and it may be a bit difficult for you to do, but it has been designed to push you to really think about your own practices and your students' motivation. If you do this activity with an open mind and a positive attitude, you might gain some valuable insights.

For this exercise, please think about a challenging assessment that you have given to your students in the past; this could be a test, a quiz, a project, or any type of assessment. Try to select an assessment that often yields some low grades for your students. In the box below, write down a brief description of this assessment.

Description of Assessment:

Next, answer the questions provided in Activity 6.6; all of your answers should refer to the assessment that you just described. And here is the tricky part—force yourself to answer each question! You can't respond with "Does not apply" or "I can't do that."

Activity 6.6 Difficult Questions About Assessment

Question	Response
If my students do not do well on this assessment, do they have an opportunity to remediate and improve their grade?	
When students do not do well on this assessment, do I provide them with specific feedback explaining why a response was incorrect, and do I offer suggestions?	

Since the students often don't do well on this assessment, what is something that I can do next year to remedy this situation?	
If I were required to give a different type of assessment for this topic, what would it be?	
Will my students want to learn more about this topic after having taken this assessment?	

Try to find a colleague with whom you can reflect on your responses. It takes a lot of courage as teachers for us to critically self-reflect on the ways that we assess student learning and to consider alternatives when needed. Yet if our end goal is to support our students' learning and to encourage future exploration of the topic, then sometimes this self-reflection can be invaluable.

SHOULD I BE NICE?

CHAPTER

7

In the United States, the average student spends 6.64 hours per day in school, which is more time in school than most students in most other OECD[1] countries (Sparks, 2019). When one considers that on average there are 180 days in the school year and that students spend twelve years in school (not even counting kindergarten), this equates to 14,342 hours in school (NCES, 2008). And students spend almost all of that time in school with their teachers. Consequently, the relationships between students and teachers are important, given that they spend so much time together.

Whereas we often focus on the purely academic functions of teachers (i.e., to support student learning), in this chapter, we'll examine the roles that teacher-student relationships play in motivation. We'll be examining how these relationships develop and how they can be nurtured. The relationships between students and teachers can support students' day-to-day motivation in the classroom, as well as longer-term motivation that affects students' future educational and professional plans.

Understanding Your Own Motivation

When we think back on our own educational experiences, we all can remember teachers with whom we had great relationships and other teachers with whom we had difficult relationships. For the next activity, you will have the opportunity to reflect on some of those relationships.

You may never have entertained the possibility that the relationships that you had with your teachers when you were a student may have impacted your motivation. Those relationships can have powerful effects on our motivation. I recall a high school language arts teacher (who was very affable and with whom many students had good relationships) who pulled me aside one day

---

[1] Organisation for Economic Co-operation and Development

Activity 7.1 Remembering Our Teachers

Think about relationships that you have had with your teachers throughout your education. Select the one K–12 teacher with whom you had what you would consider to be your most positive relationship and the one with whom you had the most negative/unpleasant relationship. Then, answer the questions below separately for each of these teacher-student relationships.

	Best Relationship	Worst Relationship
What grade level and subject did this person teach?		
What did this teacher do to make these your best and worst relationships?		
Did your relationship with this teacher affect your motivation? If so, how?		
Did you learn anything from your experiences with this teacher that has helped you in forming relationships with your own students?		

and said, "You are a good writer; I think you should take Honors Language Arts next year; I think you could be really successful in that class." Until that moment, I had never thought of myself as being particularly talented at writing; but that interaction changed my attitude—it bolstered my confidence as a writer. I accepted this challenge, and I did enroll in the honors class the next year. And I subsequently continued to develop my skills as a writer (and I still write now!). I often wonder if things would have turned out differently if my teacher had never taken the time to encourage me as a writer; I am grateful that he did.

A positive relationship with a teacher can lead to a greater confidence as a learner (i.e. Secret Sauce #1) and a greater appreciation for the content being taught (i.e., Secret Sauce #2). But as important as good relationships are, difficult relationships between students and teachers matter as well; indeed, a negative or contentious relationship with a teacher can lead to a dislike for the content that is being taught and to a decline in a student's confidence as a learner.

Your Relationships With Your Students

Let's assess your current relationships with your students. Complete the quiz provided in Activity 7.2.

Activity 7.2 Relationships With Students

Indicate how much you agree with each of the following statements by circling the appropriate number:

	Strongly Disagree	Disagree	Neither Agree nor Disagree	Agree	Strongly Agree
I tell students stories about my experiences when I was their age.	1	2	3	4	5
I talk about my family with my students.	1	2	3	4	5
I know all of my students' names.	1	2	3	4	5
I have informal conversations with all of my students at least once per week.	1	2	3	4	5
I speak individually to each of my students at least once per month about his/her academic performance.	1	2	3	4	5
I use humor while I'm teaching.	1	2	3	4	5
After weekends or school breaks, I ask my students if they had a good weekend/break.	1	2	3	4	5
After weekends or school breaks, I share with my students some of what I did during my break.	1	2	3	4	5
I make sure that all of my students feel included in my class (even the quiet ones).	1	2	3	4	5
I try to smile a lot and be friendly to my students.	1	2	3	4	5
Total: (add up your score by adding each of the numbers that you circled; maximum score is 50):					

How do you feel about your total score? If it is high, it suggests that you do things to cultivate positive interpersonal relationships with your students; if it is low, it suggests that you do not emphasize or prioritize the development of strong interpersonal relationships with your students. This is not a scientific quiz by any means, but it should give you a holistic impression of your relationships with your students. And there is no "right" or "wrong" score on this quiz—some of us interact with students more than others; the quiz was merely designed to encourage you to reflect on your own interaction styles with your students.

Caring About Our Students

Teacher-student relationships are often characterized as "caring" relationships. Teachers can express care for students through our interactions with them. But what exactly does it mean to be a "caring" teacher?

There actually are two different ways to think about teacher caring. Teachers can express care for their students by expressing care for students' well-being (i.e., psychological and physical well-being), and teachers can express care for our students with regard to their academic performance. Both of these are important, but we need to recognize that they are different.

WHAT DO CARING TEACHERS DO?

There are some core characteristics of caring teachers that cut across both types of caring. In general, caring teachers (a) listen attentively to their students, (b) think deeply about individual students' needs, and (c) work toward creating a climate of care throughout the school, such that both teachers and students care for one another (Noddings, 2012). In a classic research study, Wentzel (1997) asked several hundred middle school students to answer the question, "How do you know when a teacher cares for you?" Interestingly, the most frequent responses pertained to students' perceptions of the teacher as *caring about the student as a learner*. Students perceive teachers as caring about their learning when teachers do things such as checking to see if a student is understanding the current lesson, or recognizing the student's skills.

As teachers, we express **care with regard to academic performance** when we talk to individual students about their academic performance. We can express academic caring by taking time to discuss students' progress, asking our students if they need any help, or offering a compliment or praise to a student for a specific accomplishment. We also can express academic caring when we take the time to notice that a student is not working up to potential.

Teachers express **care with regard to students' well-being** when we take some time to talk to our students about their feelings, their health, their social lives, their families, or just about any other aspect of their lives. Students often deeply appreciate it when a teacher takes a few minutes to ask a student about her weekend or to ask a student if she is enjoying her after-school job. And sometimes, for example, we can express care about both academic and more general student well-being. A teacher who knows that a student has an after-school job might ask the student, "How are you doing with your job? Are you able to manage working those hours and also getting your schoolwork done? Anything I can do to help you figure out how to manage all of this?"

Effects of Positive Teacher-Student Relationships

There are many benefits to positive teacher-student relationships. First, as a teacher, it's more enjoyable to go to work every day when we have positive relationships with our students; similarly, it's more pleasant for the students when they know that they have good relationships with their teachers. Teacher-student relationships promote happiness in our students because these relationships support the basic psychological needs of all students that we discussed in Chapter 1 (i.e., the need for autonomy, relatedness, and competence) (Froiland, Worrell, & Oh, 2019). But in addition to creating a pleasant environment in which we can teach and students can learn, there are other tangible benefits for our students.

The effects of teacher-student relationships are positive for students across diverse ethnic and cultural groups (Cornelius-White, 2007). When teachers and students have positive, caring relationships with each other, students are more likely to concentrate on academic tasks, to exert effort, and to enjoy doing their work; in turn, this focus on academics leads to greater learning and achievement. However, when students and teachers have problematic, contentious relationships, students are less likely to attend to their work, and their achievement suffers (Roorda, Jak, Zee, Oort, & Koomen, 2017).

Positive teacher-student relationships also have some unique positive effects for some specific groups of students. For example, when young children first transition into kindergarten and the early elementary school grades, strong positive relationships with teachers support young children's social and cognitive development (Davis, 2003). Positive relationships with students can help them to develop a growth mindset, particularly in young children who are just beginning their school experiences (Foca, 2016). And for adolescents, positive teacher-student relationships are related to high achievement and attendance and to fewer occurrences of disruptive behavior, fewer school suspensions, and a lower likelihood of dropping out of school (Quin, 2007). Positive relationships can be particularly helpful for students with disabilities (Murray & Pianta, 2007) and students with attention-deficit hyperactivity disorder (Ewe, 2019). Moreover, strong relationships with teachers can diminish depressive symptoms in students who experience bullying (Huang, Lewis, Cohen, Prewett, & Herman, 2018).

MOTIVATION MYTH

Myth: *Students will learn more and be more motivated if teachers don't smile until the winter holidays.*

Truth: *Student motivation and learning are enhanced when teachers and students have good relationships with each other.*

All Are Welcome Here

When I began teaching, many of my colleagues told me, "Don't smile until Christmas." The logic behind this statement (which most teachers have heard during their careers) is that students are more likely to misbehave and less likely to cooperate if they believe that the teacher is nice and easygoing. If students think that a teacher is mean or strict, then they will behave better and work harder; therefore, if we "don't smile" for the first part of the year, students will learn to behave appropriately. Whereas this advice is well intentioned, and students might behave well out of fear of the teacher, this advice is not necessarily conducive to supporting student motivation. If you don't smile until Christmas, the students also might not smile until Christmas. That doesn't bode well for student motivation.

As we have mentioned in several chapters, student motivation is stronger and more positive when students experience autonomy, when they **do not** feel highly controlled by their teachers, and when teachers provide rationales for the types of activities that we ask our students to do (Patall & Zambrano,

2019; Reeve, 2006). When students perceive their teachers as stern and strict, they probably will behave well, but they will be deprived of experiencing autonomy, which is one of the key ingredients in promoting student motivation. So, we might want to rethink the notion of not smiling until Christmas.

PROMOTING A SENSE OF BELONGING

One of the most important ways that teachers can nurture positive relationships with their students is by promoting a sense of **belonging** in our classrooms and our schools. Students feel like they belong in their schools when they feel that they are accepted, respected, included, and supported by their peers and their teachers and school staff (Goodenow & Grady, 1993; Slaten, Ferguson, Allen, Brodrick, & Waters, 2016).

Student perceptions of school belonging are related to a wide array of positive outcomes, including greater motivation (e.g., greater self-efficacy), high grades, positive attitudes toward learning, and low levels of absenteeism, truancy, bad behavior, and dropping out of school (Allen, Kern, Vella-Brodrick, Hattie, & Waters, 2018).

One of the most important predictors of a sense of belonging among adolescents is the perception by students that they have positive relationships with their teachers; this means that they perceive their teachers to be caring, fair, and concerned about students' personal problems (Allen et al., 2018). As we discuss strategies to enhance our relationships with our students, keep in mind that when we have positive relationships with our students, we help to create a sense of belonging both for individual students with whom we have positive interactions, as well as for the larger school community—when students see that teachers are communicative and caring and promote mutual respect, this helps to create a sense of belonging throughout the school community (L. Anderman 2003).

Sometimes there are students who fall through the cracks; there are some students who don't feel as though they belong. These students may feel particularly lonely, and this can have a negative effect on their motivation, achievement, and psychological well-being (E. Anderman 2002). We need to make a concerted effort to be sure that all students feel that they belong. Activity 7.3 provides an opportunity for you to think about whether all students in your school feel that they belong.

Particularly at the middle school and high school level, some of our students who don't feel like they belong at school may not have anyone to turn to for support. Middle and high school teachers are of course very busy with many students and many responsibilities; but often these neglected students continue to be neglected. Try to keep this in mind—if nobody takes responsibility for the students who don't belong, then those students will languish and may experience decreases in achievement and motivation and an increased risk of experiencing psychological distress.

Activity 7.3 School Belonging

Despite our best efforts, there are some students in our schools who don't feel like they belong. After reading the descriptions of the types of students, think about what you could do to promote a sense of belonging for those specific students.

Descriptions of Students	What can I do to promote a sense of belonging in these students?
Students who are very timid/shy	
Students who are in special education	
Ethnically diverse students	
Religiously diverse students	
Students who identify as LGBT	
Students with same-sex parents	
Students who are adopted	
Students who seem to always sit by themselves in the cafeteria	
Students who are fostered	
Students who have physical disabilities	
Students who are not good at sports	
Students who are bullied	
Students who are bullies	
Students who often misbehave	
Students who have a parent in prison	
Students who are homeless	
Are there other students in your school who may not feel a high sense of belonging? Who are these students? What could you do to promote a sense of belonging for them?	

⚙️ STRATEGY 7.1

All students benefit from feeling a sense of belonging. Talk to all of your students and try to figure out if there are any students who truly do not feel as though they belong in the school. Consult with your colleagues, school counselors, or school social workers to develop strategies to support these students.

Teacher-Student Relationships Across the Years

There are obvious differences in the types of relationships that we develop with our students based on school configurations and grade levels. Elementary school teachers establish different types of relationships with their students than secondary teachers. Students in elementary schools spend most of their time with one teacher during most of the day, whereas students in secondary schools generally have several teachers per day and only spend a brief amount of time with each teacher. Moreover, elementary school teachers are responsible for teaching fewer students than do secondary teachers. We can have positive, caring relationships with students of all ages, but the nature of those relationships will change over time, because the amount of time that we can spend with each student changes as students move into secondary schools.

Teacher-student relationships are very important for young children, particularly when they are first starting school. For some children, this will be the first time that they are spending significant amounts of time with adults outside of the family; for other children who have attended preschool programs, the nature of the relationships with teachers in elementary schools may differ from relationships with preschool teachers. Some children may have had the opportunity to develop close, caring relationships with preschool educators, whereas others may have had preschool teachers who were caretakers, but did not develop close relationships with the children. Strong relationships with elementary school teachers support the development of positive expectancies, valuing of school and subject areas, liking school, and a growth mindset in young children (Foca, 2016). It is critical for children to develop adaptive motivational beliefs early in their school careers, as these early beliefs are predictive of subsequent motivation and achievement. Teacher-student relationships during the early elementary school years can support the development of beneficial motivational beliefs in students. From kindergarten through third grade, teacher-student interactions that (a) reflect teachers' sensitivity to the individual needs of children, (b) promote and recognize children's positive behaviors, and (c) stimulate language development and cognitive growth, are essential and help set students up for future academic success (Pianta, Downer, & Hamre, 2016).

Although there often is an assumption that teacher-student relationships are more important for younger children than for adolescents (particularly because adolescents value independence from adults), research indicates that teacher-student relationships are just as important for secondary students as they are for elementary students (Roorda et al., 2017). Nevertheless, the nature of these relationships will be different. We can have conversations with adolescents about topics that we might not address with younger children. When we recognize that adolescents are developing socially, cognitively, and emotionally, and when our communications with adolescent students reflect that recognition, we can develop positive, caring relationships with adolescent students (we'll look at some strategies for how to do this later in the chapter).

Culture, Diversity, and Teacher-Student Relationships

We need to consider culture and ethnicity in our relationships with our students. As much as we would like to think that we can easily develop positive relationships with all of our students, it isn't always quite that simple. A Black male student may not find it easy to develop a positive relationship with a White female teacher; a Muslim female student may not find it easy to develop a positive relationship with a Christian or Jewish male teacher. Supporting this, there is some evidence that Black and Latinx students are rated as better behaved and higher achieving when they are taught by a teacher of the same race or ethnicity; these relationships are stronger for students in higher grades, and for Black students who are taught by Black teachers (Redding, 2019). These observations may be attributable to the formation of stronger, more trusting relationships between teachers and students who share similar backgrounds.

This does not mean that we cannot or should not work to develop caring, trusting relationships with all students; but it does mean that we need to recognize the unique backgrounds of our students, and acknowledge, appreciate, and value those differences. There are some strategies that we can use to promote positive relationships and a sense of belonging with students from diverse backgrounds. Some of these include the following (Gray, Hope, & Matthews, 2018):

- Support diverse students by providing them with opportunities to explore and talk about their racial and ethnic identities.
- Consistently demonstrate an appreciation for and valuing of students' cultures in our instruction.

- Create a classroom in which students from diverse backgrounds can take pride in their cultures and in people who look like they do.

- Recognize that current events and societal issues may affect students from diverse backgrounds differently than for majority students; acknowledge this and talk about these issues with your students.

Strategies for Promoting Positive Teacher-Student Relationships

When you think about your interactions with students, these interactions can serve a number of purposes that are beneficial to your students. Although it isn't always natural for us to converse with our students individually, such conversations are essential in developing positive student-teacher relationships. But we have to make a commitment to developing and nurturing these relationships. When we consistently work toward developing positive relationships with our students, we are creating a context that can facilitate our use of the many strategies presented throughout the book to support students' motivation.

As we noted earlier, some of our interactions and conversations with our students may reflect academic caring, and others may reflect caring about students' overall well-being. Both types of interactions are important. Table 7.1 presents a series of "conversation starters." These are divided into conversation starters that reflect academic caring (i.e., instructional support) and caring about students' well-being (i.e., affective support) (Davis, 2006).

Try to make a commitment to use some of these conversation starters (or other conversation starters) with each of your students. Obviously, the frequency that you can have such individual conversations will depend upon the number of students that you teach and the time that you spend with your students. If you are an elementary school teacher with twenty-five students, it will of course be easier to converse with all students fairly regularly. But if you are a high school teacher with 150 students (whom you only see for fifty minutes per day), then you obviously will not be able to speak to each student daily. Nevertheless, it is possible to initiate conversations with all of your students if you approach this strategically. One method that high school teachers can use is to keep a record in our grade books indicating when we have had conversations with

Table 7.1 Conversation Starters

Here are some ideas for ways that you can initiate conversations with your students. There are many other ways to start these conversations; these are just a few examples.	
Academic Caring (Instructional Support)	"You wrote a great essay, Steven. I loved the way you used so many great descriptive adjectives. That helped make it so interesting!"
	"Hi, Tamera. Just wanted to check in with you to see how you are doing with this week's math problems. Do you need any help with anything?"
	"Jason, I was surprised that you got a 75 percent on that last assignment; that's not like you. What's up? What can I do to help?"
	"Beth, I want to make sure you really understand this unit; can you stop by after school today for 10 minutes so we can check in and see if I can clarify anything for you? It would be great if you could, just for a few minutes."
	"Asa, you did a great job with your homework last night. I really noticed how hard you worked on it."
	"George, your poster is good, but be honest with me, how much time did you spend working on it? If I let you take it home tonight, do you think you might be able to spend some more time on it? It's good, but it could be great!"
Caring About Well-Being (Affective Support)	"Sarah, I really want to thank you for your efforts in cleaning up today. I really do appreciate it."
	"What's up, Jeremy? I can tell you're sad about something."
	"Lynn, how was your weekend? Tell me about something that you did."
	"Jack, what you did to Seth on the playground was not cool. You really upset him by teasing him. Jack, you're a great kid—I really want to talk about this with you."
	"Caris, what's your favorite dessert? Mine is apple pie. What do you like?"
	"Ginger, what's your favorite TV show? Believe it or not, mine is 'The Price is Right.'"

Developed using the following sources: Davis (2006); Wentzel (1997).

each of our students (i.e., just entering some kind of indicator of when you had a one-on-one conversation with each student). If you notice that you have not had a conversation with a particular student in a long time, then by keeping a record, you will be able to make an effort to engage with that student. Sometimes we may honestly believe that we talk to all of our students regularly, but when we keep records, we often notice that we don't engage with our students as consistently as we might think that we do. Simply putting a check mark in our grade book when we have brief informal conversations with a student can serve as a great tool to help us to engage with all of our students.

SCHOOLWIDE STRATEGIES FOR PROMOTING POSITIVE TEACHER-STUDENT RELATIONSHIPS

We don't have to think about teacher-student relationships only as the dyadic relationships between a teacher and an individual student. The relationships between teachers and students also are reflective of the general climate of the school. It's great if a student has a good relationship with an individual teacher, but it's also important for students to feel that the teachers in this school care about all of them and like talking to all students. When students perceive that teachers at a school **do not** care about the students, then the students' motivation and achievement will be affected negatively.

There are strategies that can be implemented at a school-level to promote overall positive relationships between teachers and students. Some examples are provided in Table 7.2.

Table 7.2 Schoolwide Efforts to Promote Positive Teacher-Student Relationships

Strategy	Example
Learn students' first names	The teachers at North High School realize that it is going to be impossible for all teachers to learn all students' names because there are almost 2,000 students in the school; however, the teachers decide to each try to learn the students' names in one grade level (e.g., Mrs. Ryan learns the names of all of the tenth graders, and Mr. Collins learns the names of all of the eleventh graders). They facilitate this by having monthly grade-specific town hall meetings and by providing the teachers with a password-protected web page with the students' photos and names. The teachers then make an effort to greet and chat with as many students as possible (e.g., between classes, during lunch, etc.) using students' first names.
Recognize strengths in all students	The teachers at Lucas Middle School have developed a student recognition program; they ensure that every student is recognized at least once per semester in a positive way.

(Continued)

Table 7.2 (Continued)

Teachers serve as mentors and advisors	In all of the schools in Fletcher County, students belong to advisory groups that are led by a teacher; the groups meet once per week to discuss everything from current events to study strategies. This starts in elementary school and continues through high school. In the middle and high schools, a different teacher leads each discussion group every marking period, so that students develop positive relationships with a range of teachers; in the elementary schools, the students' regular classroom teacher serves in this role.
Have lunch with students	The teachers at Brookside Elementary School have lunch with their students in the cafeteria. Students learn starting in kindergarten that teachers enjoy spending time with students and having informal conversations.
Attend school events	Each of the teachers at Clay High School has committed to attending at least one extracurricular event per month (e.g., a sports event, a concert, a school play, etc.).

Summing Up

In this chapter, we have discussed the importance of teacher-student relationships. Our students will be more motivated to learn if they have positive relationships with their teachers. We can develop positive relationships in many different ways. It is particularly important for us to express that we care about our students. Caring can be communicated in terms of academic caring (i.e., caring about students' learning and progress) and general caring about students' well-being.

We need to be cognizant of the developmental level of our students and of their unique ethnic and cultural backgrounds as we nurture these relationships. We can enhance our relationships with our students when we make a concerted effort to initiate individual conversations with each of our students. Moreover, we can implement schoolwide strategies to support the development of a school climate in which students perceive that all of the teachers care about the students and want them to be successful,

APPLYING WHAT YOU HAVE LEARNED

In this chapter, we have discussed several strategies for developing positive relationships with our students. Considering all of these strategies, try to do the following:

1. Write down your thoughts about the current relationships that you have with your students. Do you think that your students see you as approachable? Do you think that they see you as a teacher who cares about their academic performance? Do you think that they see you as a teacher who cares about their general well-being?

2. Take your class list(s), and try to remember the last time that you had a positive conversation (either individually or in a small group) with each of your students.

3. Make a commitment to do something different to develop positive relationships with your students. Be specific and write down that commitment.

4. Make a plan for implementation of that commitment. How will you implement it? When will you implement it? How will you make sure that you follow through with the commitment?

WHAT ABOUT BEHAVIOR MANAGEMENT?

So far, we have been discussing the many strategies that teachers can implement to support student motivation. Many of these strategies emphasize the need to allow students to experience autonomy. Nevertheless, you have probably begun to wonder how realistic all of this is . . . how can students be afforded the opportunities to work independently and to make their own decisions, while at the same time maintaining an orderly and well-behaved classroom? That's what this chapter is about. Efforts to motivate our students often fail because they are not aligned with our efforts to manage behavior. After reading this chapter, you will hopefully have a better sense of how to both manage behavior and support your students' motivation for all that they do in your classroom.

Understanding Your Own Motivation

We have all experienced situations where we have probably felt that the rules were too strict. To put it simply, those situations are usually not fun! For this first activity, I'm going to ask you to reflect on some situations in which you may have had such experiences.

When you look back on these situations, are there strategies that the teachers or coaches could have used that would have made the experience more pleasant for you? There are many times when it is important to have stringent rules in place, but at times, these rules can become overwhelming and diminish our interest in the class or activity. In this chapter, we'll

Activity 8.1 No Fun!

For this activity, try to come up with at least one example of an experience that you had (as a student) that meets the following criteria and briefly describe what happened and how that affected your experience.

Situation	What happened? In retrospect, how did this affect your experience that year?
An elementary school class where the teacher was overly strict.	
A middle school or high school class that had too many rules and procedures . . . so many that they got in the way of your learning.	
A college or graduate school class that (a) was about a topic that you really enjoyed learning about, and that (b) was run in a way that actually diminished your interest after having taken the class.	
Being a member of a team or an organization that was driven by rules and procedures that made the experience unpleasant.	

explore this and provide strategies that you can use to avoid these complicated situations.

Why Are We Talking About Behavior Management in a Book About Motivation?

During your teacher training program, chances are that you probably did not discuss student motivation **and** behavior management simultaneously; in fact, you may not have ever discussed them in the same course—motivation and behavior management are often not thought of in terms of how they affect each other. Nevertheless, motivation and behavior management are actually intricately tied to each other.

One of the themes that has resonated through some of the previous chapters is that motivation is enhanced when students experience a sense of autonomy. Students often feel more confident about their abilities and enjoy learning more when they are able to engage in some independent work and make some independent decisions during the school day. Allowing students to experience autonomy requires the teacher to release some control. However, this creates a dilemma, because most educators believe that the more control that we maintain over our students, the more likely they are to be well behaved. This is depicted in Figure 8.1.

When we adopt a strict style of managing student behavior (e.g., we have many rules and we consistently enforce those rules by punishing students who break them), students tend to behave well. In contrast, for many (but certainly not all) teachers, when we are not particularly strict with our students (e.g., we have few or no rules, and when we do have rules, we enforce them inconsistently), students often misbehave. In terms of motivation, when we encourage our students to be independent and to make decisions regarding how they will approach their work, students tend to develop adaptive motivational beliefs (i.e., they are likely to be confident and to enjoy learning); however, when teachers are very controlling and do not afford students many opportunities to be autonomous (i.e., we make all of the decisions and implement rigid structures), students' confidence may suffer, and they may report that they do not really enjoy the subject that is being taught.

So therein lies the dilemma . . . ideally, a teacher who wants to maintain good behavior might choose to implement a strict behavior management style; however, a teacher who wants to support the development of positive motivational beliefs might

Figure 8.1 Behavior Management and Student Motivation

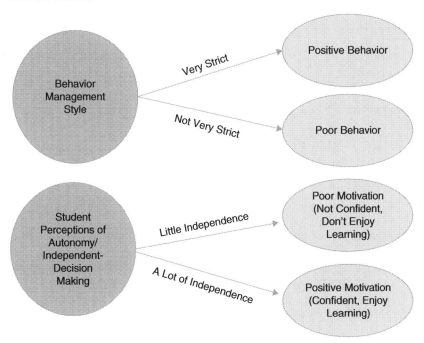

choose to allow students to work independently and to make decisions about how they will approach their work. For many of us, this creates a challenge. The big question for many teachers is the following: **How do I promote autonomy and independence and at the same time maintain enough control to manage student behavior**?

We're going to examine this big question throughout the rest of this chapter because this is extremely important, yet seldom considered (McCaslin & Good, 1992). Complicating this further, it's important to recognize that the appropriate balance between providing sufficient structure while also allowing students to have some autonomy changes as students develop (Eccles et al., 1993). As children grow older, they develop more advanced cognitive abilities, and become more able to make decisions and work independently; therefore logically, we should afford students greater opportunities for independence as they get older. However, sometimes our students' emerging abilities to think abstractly and make independent decisions conflict with the rules that we implement to manage behavior. For example, in many schools, children actually have more opportunities to be involved in classroom decision-making during the latter years of elementary school than they do after the transition into middle school. One of the reasons this occurs is because some middle school teachers believe that adolescents are more prone to misbehavior than are younger children; the assumption is that if teachers maintain control, students well be less likely to misbehave (Midgley & Feldlaufer, 1987). Although middle school students have a greater capacity to be involved in decision-making, they often have fewer opportunities to do so. This can be frustrating to early adolescents and can contribute both to boredom and to misbehavior. Mismatches between what students need and what schools provide serve as a breeding ground for low engagement, poor motivation, and misbehavior (Eccles et al., 1993).

Rules and Procedures

Let's first take a look at how we use rules and procedures to manage our students' behavior. Sometimes we develop our own rules for our classrooms; other rules might reflect schoolwide policies that apply to all students in the school. What rules do you currently have in place in your classroom and your school? Have you ever considered whether any of those rules affect your students' motivation (either positively or negatively)? Let's explore this. For Activity 8.2, list four specific rules that are enforced either by you in your classroom or throughout your

Activity 8.2 Rules and Motivation

Rules	Potential Effects on Confidence	Potential Effects on Values
1.		
2.		
3.		
4.		

entire school. For each rule, consider how the rule might have either a positive or a negative effect on your students' motivation. Try to come up with effects that the rule might have with regard to the two secret sauces (students' self-efficacy beliefs and their achievement values.) If you can think of both potential positive and negative effects, then write both down; if you can't think of any potential effects for one of the rules, then just leave that response blank. We'll return to this activity later in the chapter.

You may have found this activity to be somewhat challenging; indeed, most of us do not regularly think about how our rules for behavior management are related to our students' motivation. Nevertheless, as you will see, the rules that are in place do affect our students' motivation. Effective rules and procedures can promote good behavior by increasing engagement with tasks (Brophy & Everston, 1976). Right now, I just wanted to plant this seed with you because you may never have thought about how rules for behavior management and student motivation are related. We'll come back to this later in the chapter and offer some specific strategies.

Engagement

Until now we have been discussing student motivation. But you have probably also heard the term **engagement**. Although engagement is often used interchangeably with motivation (and is strongly related to motivation), engagement is slightly different (Eccles & Wang, 2012). And as you'll see, engagement is extremely important in terms of balancing behavior management and motivation.

WHAT EXACTLY IS "ENGAGEMENT?"

So far, we have been discussing motivation in terms of students' beliefs, values, needs, and goals; let's now look at how we define engagement (but don't worry about confusing motivation and engagement . . . as you'll see, engagement is just one part of the big picture in effective classrooms!). Just as we discovered that there are many different types of motivation (e.g., students' self-efficacy beliefs, their values, etc.), there are also different types of engagement. In general, engagement refers to the ways that students focus on various classroom tasks and activities. When students are engaged with their work, they are less likely to misbehave (because their focus is on the task or activity). There are three major types of engagement: behavioral, emotional, and cognitive engagement (Fredricks, Blumenfeld, & Paris, 2004):

Behavioral engagement is characterized by observable behaviors that students display while working on their academic tasks. The following are indicators of behavioral engagement:

- Working diligently on academic tasks (e.g., persisting, exerting effort, paying attention, actively participating in discussions)

- Appropriate classroom behavior (e.g., following rules, refraining from engaging in disruptive behavior, encouraging others to stay focused)

- Actively participating in activities (e.g., joining extracurricular activities, playing on sports teams, volunteering for school activities)

Emotional engagement is characterized by students experiencing positive affect while working on academic tasks. High emotional engagement is characterized by students experiencing positive emotions while working on academic tasks (e.g., happiness, interest, enjoying being at school, joy, having fun); in contrast, low emotional engagement is characterized by students experiencing negative emotions while engaged with their work (e.g., sadness, boredom, worry, anxiety, anger).

Cognitive engagement is characterized by students using effective strategies and approaches to learning while engaged with academic tasks. Cognitive engagement is similar to behavioral engagement, but exemplars of cognitive engagement are not necessarily easily observable (as they are with behavioral engagement). Students are cognitively engaged when they

- persist when they encounter challenging tasks;
- are invested in and committed to learning;
- cope well with failure;

- prefer challenging tasks; and
- use effective strategies (e.g., they are organized, they use effective study skills, they work hard on their homework, etc.).

HOW IS ENGAGEMENT RELATED TO MOTIVATION?

You should think of engagement as a by-product of students' motivation. Students approach academic tasks with a variety of motivational beliefs, goals, needs, and values, all of which can either support or hinder their engagement. The relationships between motivation, engagement, classroom behavior, and achievement are portrayed in Figure 8.2.

Ultimately, when students are engaged with their academic work, they will learn more; moreover, when students are engaged with their work, they also tend to be well behaved. Engagement helps to translate "motivation into effective action" (Wigfield et al., 2015, p. 671).

It's important to recognize that motivation and engagement should be considered by teachers all the time. Both motivation and engagement should be considered in our planning, and they should not be considered separately; we should plan for both every day—that's how we can support motivation and hopefully prevent disruptive behavior from occurring! In effective classrooms, students are highly motivated (i.e., they set reasonable goals, they feel able to achieve those goals, and they value the content), and because they are highly motivated, they are likely to be engaged with their work. And when they are focusing on their work, they simply don't have a lot of time to spend goofing off and misbehaving. Moreover, the engagement with their work leads to deeper learning and to higher achievement (Reeve & Tseng, 2011).

Figure 8.2 Between Motivation, Engagement, Achievement, and Behavior

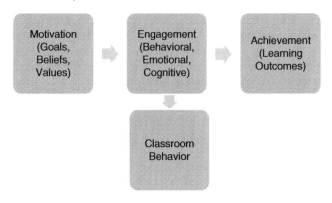

WHAT ELSE DO I NEED TO KNOW
ABOUT ENGAGEMENT?

There is a large body of research on academic engagement (Christenson, Reschly, & Wylie, 2012). When students are engaged, they are less likely to misbehave and more likely to pay attention to their work and achieve at higher levels. Some of the other significant considerations with regard to engagement include the following (Bingham & Okagaki, 2012; Christenson et al., 2012; Fredricks et al., & Paris, 2004; Rumberger & Rotermund, 2012; Wang & Eccles, 2012):

- Higher levels of engagement are related to a lower likelihood of dropping out of school.

- Engagement tends to decrease between the ages of 12–16.

- Behavioral engagement declines more than does the use of effective cognitive approaches to learning.

- Students' engagement is related to culture and ethnicity; students' experiences, beliefs, and expectations for the future affect their engagement with tasks.

- On average, students who are more engaged with their academic work experience greater overall psychological well-being than do students who are not engaged.

The takeaway message is that engagement is something that we should be promoting in classrooms. And as I mentioned earlier, don't worry about the distinction between motivation and engagement too much; that isn't really what this chapter is about; rather, my goal so far has been to introduce you to the concept of engagement (as part of the larger motivation equation) and to recognize that students who are engaged with their work are less likely to misbehave. Next, we'll turn to some strategies that you can use to promote engagement.

HOW CAN I PROMOTE ENGAGEMENT
IN MY CLASSROOM?

Let's look at some strategies that you can use to promote engagement. The strategies, along with examples, are presented in Figure 8.3.

Notice that the strategies presented in Figure 8.3 are all focused on promoting engagement through positive, affirming interactions with our students. In contrast to strategies that teachers should use to promote engagement, there is one strategy that we should avoid at all costs: **Don't mandate engagement via classroom rules**! Engagement is something that should occur naturally; students should want to be engaged. We want

Figure 8.3 Strategies to Promote Engagement

Provide academic support
- Mrs. Jones walks around her third-grade classroom several times a day to offer suggestions to students individually.
- Mr. Murphy opens his high school biology classroom up for extra help during lunch every day; he encourages everyone to stop by at least once per month.

Provide interpersonal support
- Mr. Jackson makes sure to chat with each of his fourth graders at least once per week to check in with them about their relationships with their classmates.
- Ms. Arthur brings up the topic of cyberbullying for class discussion at least once per month and tactfully reminds her students that if they witness cyberfullying, there are ways that she and others at school can help to stop this from happening.

Set clear expectations
- Mrs. Weiss provides her fifth graders with very clear expectations for their homework; she regularly reminds the students about her expectations, and she expresses great joy when students work toward meeting those expectations.
- The administrators at Hills Middle School have developed a very clear and concise list of behavioral expectations; these are posted in the hallways, and all of the teachers regularly remind students about the expectations during their classes.

Provide opportunites for autonomy
- The teachers at Bradley Elementary School have developed a schoolwide plan that permits students to make more choices (about how they will do their work, about what books they will read, etc.) each year as students move into the next grade.
- Mrs. McVie used to set strict rules for behavior in her tenth-grade social studies classes; she has now moved to a system where she and the students develop the rules (and the consequences for not following the rules) collaboratively at the beginning of each year.

Recognize that engagement is related to culture and ethnicity
- Mrs. Portman has just started teaching second grade at a new school. Since over half of the students are Somali, she makes sure to incorporate aspects of Somali culture into all aspects of her teaching.
- Mr. Collins asks his high school language arts students to complete anonymous questionnaires at the start of the year; he asks them questions about their family backgrounds and cultural heritages. He uses that information to select short stories that the class reads throughout the year that reflect the diverse backgrounds of his students.

Developed using the following sources: Bingham & Okagaki (2012); Connell (1990); Connell & Wellborn (1991); Fredricks et al. (2004); Marks (2000); Wentzel (1997).

to avoid (if possible) situations where we punish students for not being engaged (understanding that sometimes the use of punishment may be warranted, in certain situations).

Summing Up Engagement

In this section, we introduced the notion of engagement, noting that students can be engaged behaviorally, cognitively, or emotionally. When students are motivated to learn, they are more likely to be engaged; and when students are engaged with their work, they are focusing on their work and less likely to misbehave. By doing all that we can do to promote engagement, we are creating classroom contexts that are not conducive to misbehavior.

Proactive or Reactive?

Sometimes we need to respond to inappropriate behaviors as soon as they occur. But for many of us, this becomes habitual—we wait for something bad to happen, and then deal with it after it has occurred. Following our discussion of engagement, you now hopefully can see that we can be proactive and try to prevent bad behaviors from occurring in the first place. Recall that in the discussion of academic engagement, I pointed out that academic engagement is greater in classrooms that are **not** characterized by high levels of teacher control and use of punishments. In Activity 8.3a, a series of incidents involving student behavior are presented. For each of these, think about a strategy that the teacher could have utilized **before the incident had occurred** (i.e., proactively) to promote student engagement and to hopefully have prevented this from ever occurring.

Were you able to come up with some ideas? There are many ways that these incidents could have been prevented; and we also have to be realistic. Sometimes events like these can't be prevented. But if at the beginning of the year we take a proactive stance on both behavior management and motivation, and if we follow through with this stance throughout the year, then

Activity 8.3a Being Proactive

Incident	What could the teacher have done proactively to possibly prevent this?
Jason (third grader) is working with four other students in a small group; the group is reading and talking about a short story. Jason is not paying attention and is goofing off and distracting the others in his group.	
Jenna (seventh grader) keeps taking out her phone in class and using it during a math lesson; she tries to hide it, but it is quite obvious to the teacher and to others that Jenna is either texting or playing some game.	
Frank (eleventh grader) always misbehaves in band class. He distracts other students, and whenever the teacher attempts to redirect Frank, he says things like "I hate band" or "Band sucks. I'm just in this because my parents made me take band."	

some misbehavior can be avoided, and we can enhance motivation. Adopting a positive, enthusiastic approach to all that we do in our classrooms, including managing student behavior, can both prevent misbehavior and can enhance motivation (Conoley & Conoley, 2009). Below are some examples of proactive strategies that the teachers might have used in these situations (and these are just three examples; there are many other possibilities).

Activity 8.3b Being Proactive

Incident	What could the teacher have done proactively to possibly prevent this?
Jason (third grader) is working with four other students in a small group; the group is reading and talking about a short story. Jason is not paying attention and is goofing off and distracting the others in his group.	Jason's teacher could have organized reading groups based on students' interests, so Jason could be reading a story that is more engaging. It may not always be possible or feasible to allow students to choose topics for reading, but even if students can do this once in a while, it can improve their attitudes toward reading and encourage them to stay on task and be less likely to misbehave.
Jenna (seventh grader) keeps taking out her phone in class using it during a math lesson; she tries to hide it, but it is quite obvious to the teacher and to others that Jenna is either texting or playing some game.	Jenna's teacher could have had a rule in place from the beginning of the year regarding when, where, and how phones can be used, and she should consistently enforce this rule with all students. Schools have different policies about phone usage, but if phones are allowed, then consider allocating a specific time period when students can use their phones; your students may be less likely to try to "sneak" in some phone time if they know that there is a designated time when they can use them.
Frank, who plays the trombone, always misbehaves in band class. He distracts other students, and whenever the teacher attempts to redirect Frank, he says things like "I hate band" or "Band sucks. I'm just in this because my parents made me take band."	The band teacher could ask students at the beginning of the year why they enrolled in band and assess how much they actually value band. If a student is in an elective class (like band) and is really not interested in the class, it might be worthwhile to meet with the parents or a school counselor to see if the student can perhaps choose a different class that is better aligned with the student's interests and goals. Sometimes parents are not aware of their children's true feelings about academic subjects. If it isn't possible to move the student to a different class, then assessing the student's interest in the subject at the beginning of the year can help you to plan activities that might be more engaging (and less conducive to misbehavior) for that student. For example, if Frank doesn't enjoy playing the trombone, but does enjoy using computers, perhaps Frank can be excused from playing one piece and can be assigned the task of developing a spreadsheet to keep track of the band's fundraising efforts.

STRATEGY 8.1

At the end of each day, spend a moment or two reflecting on situations in which you were reactive, but in hindsight could have been proactive. Consider how you might do something slightly differently tomorrow because of this.

REVISITING REWARDS

We're going to start this section with an activity. For Activity 8.4, consider the following scenario.

Activity 8.4 What's the Problem?

Mr. Adler is a first-year middle school teacher. Mark, one of the seventh-grade boys in his fourth-period class, often misbehaves. Mark constantly whispers to others, giggles, and encourages other students to give Mr. Adler a hard time; the other students always laugh when Mark does this—the students then stop paying attention to the lesson because they are quite entertained by Mark. Mr. Adler had thought that he had implemented an effective strategy for behavior management; he set up a system where the students get a warning after their first behavioral offense; they then lose five points for the day if they have a second offense; if they have a third offense, they lose an additional five points; and if they have a fourth offense, they receive an after-school detention. This system works fairly well with most of Mr. Adler's students, but it simply does not work with Mark. Mark regularly misbehaves at least four times per day, and he makes regular appearances at after-school detention. Mr. Adler is truly frustrated; he doesn't understand why his system works with most students, but not with Mark.

Why do you think that Mr. Adler's system is working with most students, but not with Mark? Write your response below:

There are many reasons why Mr. Adler's system may not be working in Mark's case. Mr. Adler decided to consult with some other more experienced colleagues about this. Then Mr. Adler had an epiphany: Mr. Adler suddenly realized that the "reward" of receiving so much attention from all of his classmates was incredibly valuable to Mark; it was worth it to Mark to lose points and go to detention (day after day) because he valued the attention so much. Once Mr. Adler realized this, he implemented a very effective solution. Instead of using his standard system of penalties, he decided that as soon as Mark misbehaved, he would send Mark out of the room and had Mark sit at a desk in the hallway for ten minutes; Mr. Adler would increase the duration of time out of the room for repeat offenses on the same day (e.g., to fifteen minutes for the second offense). By doing this, he immediately cut off the reinforcement that Mark was receiving from his classmates. Mr. Adler also put some colored paper up over the window on the door to his classroom so that Mark couldn't peek into the room (because he suspected that Mark would peek in and others would watch and that this would distract everyone else and further reinforce Mark's behavior).

After the first infraction, Mr. Adler sent Mark out for ten minutes; after the ten minutes, when Mark came back into the room, Mark immediately acted out and the other students laughed; Mr. Adler once again immediately sent Mark out, this time for fifteen minutes. When Mark came back in, he looked rather annoyed, and he just sat at his desk and did not engage with anyone for the duration of the class.

The next day, Mark tried again to be disruptive during the first five minutes of class; Mr. Adler again immediately sent him out of the room. This process endured for the next few days, but eventually, Mr. Adler was sending Mark out of the room less often, because Mark was misbehaving less often. Every few weeks, Mark would try once again to give Mr. Adler a hard time, and Mr. Adler immediately sent him out of the room. Eventually, Mark stopped harassing Mr. Adler. Once Mark was no longer reinforced by his classmates, his bad behavior stopped.

This scenario is quite typical . . . we often don't realize that while we think that we are doing our best to curb misbehavior, there are other things going on in the classroom and in the student's life that may hinder our efforts. And there simply may be a reward that the student is receiving (e.g., recognition from peers for giving the teacher a hard time) that is more valuable to the student than any punishment. It's not easy to assess these situations; they are usually nuanced and very complicated. When situations like this arise, it often is a good idea to consult with colleagues, a school psychologist, or school social worker, because they are trained to specifically support teachers in these situations. Nevertheless, it is important to deal with these situations and to maintain an emphasis on promoting motivation and engagement.

Take some time once per week to consider whether any rewards or reinforcers that you use (either deliberately or inadvertently) might not be affecting student behavior as you had intended.

Supporting Student Motivation While Managing Behavior

There are many strategies that teachers can use to proactively promote motivation and effectively manage student behavior. These are displayed, along with examples, in Table 8.1.

Table 8.1 Strategies That Promote Good Behavior and Student Motivation

Ensure that students are provided with clear and easily understood expectations for all tasks.	Mrs. Garbo puts expectations for all assignments on the whiteboard and reviews them daily to make sure everyone understands and to see if anyone needs help.
Deal with inappropriate behaviors immediately and consistently.	Mr. Hanley does not allow students to do work from other classes during his math class unless they have finished all of the work for his class; as soon as he sees someone working on work from another class when they should be working on algebra, he takes the student's other work away and returns it after class has ended. He reminds the students that they are permitted to do other work after their math work is completed (emphasizing that they do have some control [autonomy] in the situation).
Focus on the positive—try not to express disapproval too often.	Mrs. Murphy asked the assistant principal to make a video of her class. When Mrs. Murphy watched the video, she realized that she was expressing disapproval of student behavior on average at least twelve times per hour; she then decided to work with the assistant principal to try out some more positive approaches.
Promote a sense of community in the classroom.	Mr. Wylie uses many small-group activities in his classroom. He spends a lot of time talking to his students about the benefits of knowing how to work cooperatively in groups. He carefully organizes the groups to make sure that everyone is included and appreciated. He also demonstrates and practices conflict-resolution techniques for his students, so that they can manage any conflicts effectively and humanely.

Walk around the classroom and check in with students to make sure that they are on task; provide support when needed.	During her science classes, Mrs. Levy walks around the room and checks in regularly with each lab group. This helps her to ensure that the groups stay focused. When a group encounters a problem, she comes right over to help, so that the students don't become frustrated or start to misbehave.
Introduce novel instructional practices from time to time (students get bored doing the same thing every day!), while ensuring that your basic classroom routines remain in place.	Mr. Loman brings his fifth graders to the computer lab to work with some new math software; however, he reminds them that students must work independently and not distract each other, just as he would expect during a regular lesson in the regular classroom.
Make sure that students understand rules and procedures, but be careful not to have too many; set rules and procedures at the beginning of the year and implement them consistently.	Miss Clark has three rules in place in her third-grade classroom; she goes over these at least twice per week: Follow directions. Respect your classmates. Raise your hand and ask for help whenever you need it.
Design the layout of your classroom so that it allows for movement.	Mr. Leonard used to always arrange his eighth-grade math classroom so that the desks were in straight rows of five desks per row; he realized that he could not easily walk around and help students, and he also realized that this was not conducive to collaborative problem solving, so he re-arranged the room into small clusters of four desks, with two facing the other two.
Try to ensure that you relate what the students are learning to the real world; this is a great way to prevent students from becoming bored and losing focus.	While working on a unit on genetics in her biology class, Mrs. Lombado asks her students if they have ever heard about GMOs (genetically modified organisms), and engages them in a discussion about products that use GMOs, and how that is related to their study of genetics.
Consider the developmental appropriateness of classwork.	Mrs. Evans noticed that her students misbehave most often when they are doing worksheets. She realized that her middle school students might be more engaged (and less likely to misbehave) if they were doing more interesting and challenging work. Therefore, she limited the worksheets to only one day per week and provided her students with more challenging applied activities on the other days.
Recognize and incorporate aspects of your students' ethnic and cultural backgrounds into instruction.	Mrs. Angyal loves to come up with creative math problems. She includes examples of and references to her students' diverse backgrounds in almost all of these problems.

(Continued)

Table 8.1 (Continued)

Make sure that you are comfortable with the curriculum that you are teaching. You can focus more on engaging your students when you do not have to spend time thinking about the content or your methods during class.	Mr. King realized that his knowledge of U.S. geography was not as good as it probably should be. During a unit on westward expansion of the United States, he stumbled a few times and had to think about the geography of the west to make sure he was accurate. He decided to spend some time over summer reviewing this material, so that he would be more proficient with it next year.
Allow students to make some decisions, even if they are small, trivial ones.	Mrs. Springer makes sure that her second graders have the opportunity to be involved in decision-making at least twice per day. For example, sometimes they can choose where they will sit; sometimes they can choose which of two activities they'd like to do first; and sometimes they can choose what they'd like for a snack.
During full class lessons, make sure that students understand that they are expected to respond to questions immediately; when students realize that this is your expectation, they will stay more focused on the lesson and will be less likely to become distracted.	Mr. Lindsey regularly reminds his students that he expects them to be paying attention so they can respond to his questions; he tells them that it's okay if they aren't sure of the answer, but they do need to respond quickly.

Developed using the following sources: Anderman (2002); Graham & Taylor (2002); Lorain (2019); Pas, Cash, O'Brennan, Debnam, & Bradshaw (2015); Roorda, Jak, Zee, Oort, & Koomen (2017); Wigfield et al. (2015); Zimmer-Gembeck, Chipeur, & Hanisch (2006).

MOTIVATION MYTH

Myth: *Behavior management and motivation are unrelated—one really has nothing to do with the other.*

Truth: *Student behavior in the classroom is strongly related to motivation—when students enjoy working on academic tasks and are engaged with their classwork, they are less likely to misbehave.*

Summing Up

Take a moment and look back at your responses to activity in Activity 8.2 (Rules and Motivation). Now that we have examined the relationships between managing student behavior and student motivation, have your responses changed at all? Are you now able to complete the activity and come up with responses that you couldn't easily think of before reading this chapter?

In this chapter, I have tried to emphasize the critical need to balance our management of student behavior with our support of student motivation. The aims of managing behavior often at first glance don't align well with many of the practices that we have discussed throughout this book with regard to student motivation. Nevertheless, with thoughtful planning, this does not have to be the case.

Quite often students misbehave because they are either bored with or not enjoying the topic that you are teaching. Although much of this book focuses on strategies that you can use to support your students' motivation, there will inevitably be some topics that they simply won't enjoy learning about (Brophy, 2010). In these situations, one of the best things that you can do is to acknowledge how they feel and try to explain to them why the content is important (Deci & Ryan, 1994).

I emphasized in particular that the most effective ways to both have a well-managed classroom and to support student motivation involve the following:

- Be proactive rather than reactive whenever possible, with regard to managing student behavior.

- Be thoughtful about rules and procedures and take the time to think through the ways that those rules and procedures might thwart your efforts to support your students' motivation.

- Keep student engagement and motivation at the forefront of your planning every day. When students are engaged with their academic work, they are less likely to misbehave.

💡 APPLYING WHAT YOU HAVE LEARNED

Let's fast-forward to the beginning of the next academic year. What might you do at the beginning of next year to organize your class so that you will both maximize your students' motivation and engagement, and minimize the likelihood that they will misbehave? Use the questions provided in Activity 8.5 to consider some innovations for next year.

Activity 8.5 Changes for Next Year

Question to consider	What might you do differently?
Is there a better way of arranging the physical layout of your classroom?	
What rules will you present to the students at the start of school?	
How might you incorporate your students' cultural and ethnic backgrounds into lessons throughout the year?	
Are there some classroom activities/tasks that you know are boring? Can you think of a way of replacing at least some of these with a more creative activity?	
What is one strategy that you can introduce to try to be more proactive and less reactive with regard to behavior management?	

HOW DO I MAKE THIS ALL WORK?

Throughout this book we have been discussing the many strategies that teachers can implement to support student motivation. Hopefully the logic behind using these strategies makes sense to you, and you'll want to implement many of these strategies in your classroom. In this chapter, we're going to take a look back at some of what has been discussed. In addition, we'll look at some strategies that you can use to integrate these practices into your daily instructional plans.

Remember That Quiz?

In the introductory chapter, I asked you to take a brief quiz about motivation. Take a look back at that quiz and notice in particular any items that you answered incorrectly. Let's revisit that quiz (now that you have read this book) and discuss the answers to each question. The quiz is presented again in Table 9.1, along with the correct answers, which are highlighted.

Table 9.1 Revisiting the Motivation Quiz

Questions	Answers		
1. When teachers reward their students for completing an assignment, students will be even more motivated to complete another similar assignment.	TRUE	FALSE	IT DEPENDS
2. If a student has reached high school and is thoroughly convinced that she/he can't learn a foreign language, there isn't much hope of changing that student's mind.	TRUE	FALSE	IT DEPENDS

(Continued)

Table 9.1 (Continued)

3. If a student doesn't like a specific subject area (e.g., chemistry), the student won't be motivated in that class.	TRUE	FALSE	IT DEPENDS
4. A student can both enjoy doing a task and be motivated to get a good grade on the task.	TRUE	FALSE	IT DEPENDS
5. Motivation changes as children move from elementary school into middle school and high school.	TRUE	FALSE	IT DEPENDS
6. Whenever you test students on content, you are harming their motivation to learn that content.	TRUE	FALSE	IT DEPENDS
7. Student motivation is influenced by the people with whom a student interacts while working on a task.	TRUE	FALSE	IT DEPENDS
8. If a student is highly interested in a particular subject area (e.g., science), the student is likely to learn a lot and get good grades in that subject area.	TRUE	FALSE	IT DEPENDS
9. Students are motivated by competition	TRUE	FALSE	IT DEPENDS
10. Students will learn more and be more motivated to continue studying about a topic if we match our instructional methods with the students' preferred learning styles.	TRUE	FALSE	IT DEPENDS

Question 1. When teachers reward their students for completing an assignment, students will be even more motivated to complete another similar assignment.

Answer: It depends.

Recall that in Chapter 5, we discussed the use of rewards, acknowledging that rewards can be effective as motivators, but only in certain circumstances. If students are given a reward for merely completing an assignment (or for completing it within a specific period of time), then the students will associate the reward with having merely completed the assignment, *and not with what they actually might have learned*. Think about this— they are being rewarded for completing some work (regardless of whether or not they learned anything)—and this does not encourage students to think about or try to learn the material in a deep and meaningful way (or to want to learn more about the topic in the future). The reward simply encourages them to complete their assignments (regardless of whether or not they have learned something). However, if students are given rewards for having demonstrated that they truly learned something as a result of having completed the assignment, then the reward won't undermine their future motivation for similar tasks.

Question 2. If a student has reached high school and is thoroughly convinced that she/he can't learn a foreign language, there isn't much hope of changing that student's mind.

Answer: False.

As we discussed in Chapter 3, students often seem unmotivated to study a particular topic because they do not have confidence (i.e., self-efficacy beliefs) in their abilities in that area (Secret Sauce #1). A student who perhaps took a first-year French or Spanish class and did badly in that class might believe that she or he is simply not cut out to learn languages. However, as we pointed out, if students are able to slowly build up their confidence, then their efficacy will increase. Students who have little confidence in their ability in a particular area often can come to see that they can actually be successful in that area if future instruction is designed to help students to acquire this confidence. And remember that one of the best ways to do that is to help the student set short-term, reachable goals (rather than just focusing on long-term goals). If a student took French I and had a bad experience, but then took Spanish I and learned in a classroom in which the teacher (a) helped the students to set short-term goals, and (b) provided the students with supportive feedback throughout the week as they work toward reaching those goals, then the student would likely experience success and discover that learning a foreign language is entirely possible.

Question 3. If a student doesn't like a specific subject area (e.g., chemistry), the student won't be motivated in that class.

Answer: It depends.

Recall that in Chapter 4, we discussed achievement values (the second secret sauce). We pointed out that achievement values consist of students' beliefs about whether a subject (or task, or activity), is perceived as (a) interesting or fun, (b) important, or (c) useful. A student might not like studying chemistry (i.e., the student might not think it's fun to learn chemistry), but the student might still believe that chemistry is useful and therefore still be motivated to learn the material. When we as teachers take the time to design our lessons so that they spark student interest and they are perceived by our students as important and useful, we promote intrinsic motivation. Moreover, since achievement values are related to students' later careers choices (Lauermann, Tsai, & Eccles, 2017), when we promote positive achievement values, we help our students to not necessarily rule out certain career paths simply because they perceive content to be boring or not useful.

Question 4. A student can both enjoy doing a task and be motivated to get a good grade on the task.

Answer: Absolutely!

The answer to this question was true. Students can be motivated to learn about a topic because it is interesting (i.e., they can be intrinsically motivated), but at the same time students can understand that their test scores are important and they can work hard to get good grades (i.e., they also can be extrinsically motivated).

Question 5. Motivation changes as children move from elementary school into middle school and high school.

Answer: True.

Motivation changes in many ways over the years. As school contexts change (e.g., grades and test scores become more important in secondary school than they were in elementary school), our students' motivation often becomes more extrinsic and less intrinsic. Students' experiences with various academic subjects over the years also shape their self-perceptions of ability—if a student repeatedly experiences frustration and failure in a particular subject area (e.g., reading), that will affect the student's future motivation in that area.

Question 6. Whenever you test students on content, you are harming their motivation to learn that content.

Answer: It depends.

When teachers test students on a topic but provide little feedback when the students do poorly on those tests, the students' motivation to pursue further study about that topic is likely to diminish. However, when teachers (a) design the tests so that grades are based on demonstrating mastery (rather than just being based on the number of questions answered correctly), and (b) provide students with helpful feedback, motivation can actually be enhanced.

Question 7. Student motivation is influenced by the people with whom a student interacts while working on a task.

Answer: True.

In Chapter 2, we discussed the influences that peers, teachers, parents, and society have on our students' motivation. The expectations, beliefs, behaviors, and values of the individuals with whom our students interact have a great influence on their motivation. Moreover, it is important to recognize that many of our students' interactions with their peers in particular occur via social media; thus, these social influences on students' academic motivation don't only occur via face-to-face interactions.

Question 8. If a student is highly interested in a particular subject area (e.g., science), the student is likely to learn a lot and get good grades in that subject.

Answer: It depends.

When students are interested in a topic, they are likely to want to learn more about that topic. But we need to remember that interest is not the sole determinant of our students' motivation and learning. A student who is very interested in a topic but also has low self-efficacy with regard to that topic (i.e., the student isn't very confident in his or her ability to learn about the topic) may not get good grades when that topic is assessed, despite being interested. And a student who is interested in a topic but who is repeatedly tested on the topic with fill-in-the-blank and rote memorization assessments may grow bored with the topic over time.

Question 9. Students are motivated by competition.

Answer: It depends.

Competition can be motivating, but competitions often are only fun for those who win. When competitions are used in academic settings and the same students always win (and the same students always lose), then competition may be motivational for the high achievers, but can be devastating for the lower achieving students. Moreover, competition can induce unnecessary anxiety in students who already may be anxious about their performance in a particular class or subject area; those students may become more focused on avoiding "looking dumb" than on enjoying the activity and truly learning something.

Question 10. Students will learn more and be more motivated to continue studying about a topic if we match our instructional methods with the students' preferred learning styles.

Answer: False.

As we discussed in Chapter 5, learning "styles" are really just learning "preferences." We all prefer to do things in certain ways, but the way that we might prefer to do something isn't always the best choice. Despite the enormous popularity of learning styles, research very clearly demonstrates that adjusting our instructional methods to match students' preferred learning styles is not related to improved learning (Rogowsky, Calhoun,

& Tallal, 2015). Of course, it's great when we are aware of how our students prefer to learn, but as teachers, we need to ensure that our students are able to learn via multiple modalities, not just in their favorite ways.

Be the Bravest

Most teachers want to promote positive motivation in their students, but many of us approach this in a piecemeal fashion. We might at times choose to focus on one aspect of motivation (e.g., promoting positive relationships in our classrooms), but be unable to address the many other aspects that we've discussed. I'll be the first to admit that it is difficult to consider all of the many aspects of motivation covered in this book all the time.

Nevertheless, if we want to motivate all of our students, then we need to try to address the many facets of motivation that we've discussed as often as we can. Keep in mind that most of these strategies are easy to implement and do not involve excessive planning or purchasing of expensive new materials. I'd like to present a strategy that you might find useful to help you to think about how you can attend to multiple aspects of motivation daily.

We're going to use the word "**BRAVEST**" as an acronym to help you to think about how you can promote positive motivation in your classroom every day (see Table 9.2). The acronym represents the following categories:

B	**B**ehavior
R	**R**elationships
A	**A**utonomy
V	**V**alue
E	**E**fficacy
S	**S**haring
T	**T**esting

Implementing the BRAVEST Strategy. Hopefully you are "motivated" to motivate your students and to implement the strategies discussed in this book. But inevitably, other priorities will arise, and despite your best intentions, you may not be

Table 9.2 BRAVEST Motivation Domains

Table 9.2 includes a brief review why each of these is included in the acronym as well as the chapters in which these aspects of motivation were discussed.

	Domain	Chapters	This is related to student motivation because . . .
B	Behavior	8	. . . students can be expected to **behave** appropriately and respectfully in class and still be highly motivated and engaged.
R	Relationships	2, 7	. . . motivation is enhanced when we promote positive **relationships** between ourselves and our students, as well as between students.
A	Autonomy	1, 2, 4, 8	. . . students are more motivated when they are able to make some choices or be involved in some decision-making (i.e., they feel **autonomous**).
V	Value	4	. . . students will be more motivated and learn more when they perceive the content as being **valuable** (i.e., important, useful, and enjoyable).
E	Efficacy	3	. . . students will be more motivated when they feel confident that they can do the work we assign, understand the material we present, and get help when they need it (i.e., they have high self-**efficacy**).
S	Sharing	5	. . . the ways that we present and **share** new content with our students can either promote or diminish their motivation.
T	Testing	6	. . . **testing** and assessments often lead to fear and anxiety for our students, particularly when they do not do well on those assessments.

able to think about some of the small things that you can do on a daily basis to support student motivation.

That's where Table 9.3 comes in. Table 9.3 contains the BRAVEST rubric, along with a guiding question for each domain. I suggest that you put a copy of Table 9.2 in a prominent place where you will see it daily; this will remind you about these domains and encourage you to think about something that you can do right away to support your students' motivation.

The BRAVEST acronym is a tool that can be used in daily or weekly planning. It will be most effective if you use it daily to decide upon strategies that you can incorporate into your teaching each day. An easy-to-use planning form is provided in the Appendix. I encourage teachers to complete this form once per day (either in the morning right before you teach or at the end of the day while planning for the next day). It takes no more

Table 9.3 BRAVEST Rubric and Guiding Questions

	Domain	Daily Question to Ask Yourself
B	Behavior	*What will I do today to promote good behavior without diminishing my students' motivation?*
R	Relationships	*What will I do today to promote positive relationships in my classroom?*
A	Autonomy	*What will I do today to allow students to make some choices or be involved in some decision-making?*
V	Value	*What will I do today to help my students see today's lesson as interesting or important or useful?*
E	Efficacy	*What will I do today to help my students to feel confident about being able to learn the material that we are covering today?*
S	Sharing	*What will I do today to share new information in a manner that motivates my students?*
T	Testing	*What will I do today with regard to testing/assessment so that I reduce my students' anxiety and increase their confidence?*

than two or three minutes per day to complete the planning form. *The investment of those two or three minutes of your time daily could end up saving you enormous amounts of time during the school day*—when strategies that support student motivation are implemented regularly and consistently, students will be more engaged, better behaved, more interested in learning, and they'll achieve at higher levels.

OTHER STRATEGIES

If you don't like using rubrics like "BRAVEST," there are many other strategies that you can consider using in order to support your students' motivation. The most important point to remember is that you, as the teacher, make a difference every day in your students' lives. *It's the little things that we do that affect motivation—how we arrange groups, whether we ever let our students make some decisions, how we provide feedback, and so forth.* The minute or two that you take to encourage one of your students could make a tremendous difference in that student's life!

In Table 9.4, I offer some reminders of little things that you can do every day to support your students' motivation. The reminders in this table do not represent an exhaustive list of strategies; they are just ideas to spark you to think about the many things that you can do every day to motivate your students. You also might consider hanging up a copy of this where you will see it often as a reminder of easily implemented strategies to support student motivation.

Table 9.4 Examples of Simple Strategies That Can Be Used Daily

	Examples of Strategies
Increasing Students' Self-Efficacy	• Help students to set short-term, reachable goals and not to only focus on long-term, distant goals. • Provide students with supportive and specific feedback as often as possible. • Demonstrate ("model") problem-solving techniques.
Getting Students to Value the Content	• Ask your students about their interests and try to incorporate those into lessons whenever possible. • Incorporate fantasy elements into instruction. • Use TV, video, and social media to illustrate points when appropriate. • Choose interesting and engaging reading materials . . . if you'd be bored reading it, chances are your students would be too! • Provide examples of how content that you are teaching is used in the real-world (e.g., in various professions).
Maintaining Student Engagement	• Mix things up—don't teach exactly the same way every day. • Be flexible with grouping—don't always resort to grouping students by ability. • Use rewards cautiously—students should receive rewards when they understand that they have accomplished something or mastered a new skill; don't give rewards for merely completing work. • Don't use competition too often; it's fun to win, but it's not fun to lose, and often the same students lose repeatedly.
Testing and Assessment	• Don't talk about tests all the time! • Allow students who don't do well on a test to retake the test. • Allow students to take a test when they feel ready to take the test. • Think carefully about the questions that you put on a test . . . is the test just about memorizing facts? Will your students remember any of those facts next year? • Don't announce or share students' grades publicly. • Don't share distributions of class test scores with your students; encourage them to engage in self-comparisons, not comparisons with other students. • Focus on the importance of truly learning the material (i.e., remind students about why the content is important). • Make sure that students receive appropriate feedback so that they understand why they made mistakes on a test.
Relationships	• Learn all of your students' names. • Make sure to speak individually with every student as often as possible. • Make sure that each student knows that you understand his or her learning needs.

(Continued)

Table 9.4 (Continued)

	Examples of Strategies
	• Promote a sense of belonging among all students in your classroom. • Sit with your students at lunch from time to time. • Chat with your students in the hallways either before or after school or while transitioning between classes or activities.
Managing Behavior	• Focus on the positive—always think about how you can keep your students engaged and motivated, not just on how to deter bad behavior once it occurs. • Allow students to make some decisions and have some choices during the day. • Consider ways to make the content engaging (cognitively, emotionally, and behaviorally engaging). • Be consistent in your expectations for how students should behave—don't play favorites!

APPENDIX

DAILY MOTIVATION PLANNING

	Domain	Daily Question
B	Behavior	What will I do today to promote good behavior without diminishing my students' motivation?
R	Relationships	What will I do today to promote positive relationships in my classroom?
A	Autonomy	What will I do today to allow students to make some choices or be involved in some decision-making?
V	Value	What will I do today to help my students see today's lesson as interesting or important or useful?
E	Efficacy	What will I do today to help my students to feel confident about being able to learn?
S	Sharing	What will I do today to share new information in a manner that motivates my students?
T	Testing	What will I do today with regard to testing/assessment so that I reduce my students' anxiety and increase their confidence?

REFERENCES

Allen, K., Kern, M. L., Vella-Brodrick, D., Hattie, J., & Waters, L. (2018). What schools need to know about fostering school belonging: A meta-Analysis. *Educational Psychology Review*, *30*(1), 1–34.

Anderman, E. M. (2002). School effects on psychological outcomes during adolescence. *Journal of Educational Psychology*, *94*(4), 795–809.

Anderman, E. M. (2007). The effects of personal, classroom, and school goal structures on academic cheating. In E.M. Anderman & T. B. Murdock (Eds.), *Psychological perspectives on academic cheating* (pp. 87–106). San Diego, CA: Elsevier.

Anderman, E. M., Jensen, J., Haleman, D., & Goldstein, B. (2002). Motivation to improve adult education in undereducated adults in rural communities. In D. McInierney & S. Van Etten (Eds.), *Sociocultural influences on motivation* (Vol. 2, pp. 183–206). Greenwich, CT: Information Age Publishing.

Anderman, E. M., & Maehr, M. L. (1994). Motivation and schooling in the middle grades. *Review of Educational Research*, *64*, 287–309.

Anderman, E. M., & Wolters, C. (2006). Goals, values, and affect. In P. Alexander & P. Winne (Eds.), *Handbook of educational psychology* (2nd ed., pp. 369–390). Mahwah, NJ: Lawrence Erlbaum.

Anderman, L. H. (2003). Academic and social perceptions as predictors of change in middle school students' sense of belonging. *Journal of Experimental Education, 72*, 5–22.

Austin, J. T., & Vancouver, J. B. (1996). Goal constructs in psychology: Structure, process, and content. *Psychological Bulletin, 120*(3), 338–375. https://doi.org/ 10.1037/0033-2909.120.3.338

Bandura, A. (1997). *Self-efficacy: The exercise of control.* New York, NY: W.H. Freeman.

Bandura, A. (2019). Applying theory for human betterment. *Perspectives on Psychological Science, 14*(1), 12–15.

Bangert-Drowns, R.L., Kulik, C.C., & Kulik, J.A. (1991). The instructional effect of feedback in test-like events. *Review of Educational Research, 61*, 213–238.

Bardach, L., Oczlon, S., Pietschnig, J., & Lüftenegger, M. (2019). Has achievement goal theory been right? A meta-analysis of the relation between goal structures and personal achievement goals. *Journal of Educational Psychology.* https://doi-org.proxy.lib.ohio-state.edu/10.1037/edu0000419.supp

Barksdale, M. A., & Triplett, C. F. (2010). Valuing children's voices. *Current Issues in Education, 13*(4). Retrieved from http://cie.asu.edu/

Barnes, E. & Puccioni, J. (2017). Shared book reading and preshcool children's academic achievement: Evidence from the Early Childhood Longitudinal Study. *Infant and Child Development, 26(6),* 1–19.

Baumrind, D. (1991). Parenting styles and adolescent development. In R. Lerner, A. C. Petersen, & J. Brooks-Gunn (Eds.), *The encyclopedia of adolescence* (pp. 746–758). New York, NY: Garland Press.

Baumrind, D. (2005). Patterns of parental authority and adolescent autonomy. In J. Smetana (Ed.), *Changing boundaries of parental authority during adolescence* (pp. 61–69). San Francisco, CA: Jossey-Bass.

Beck, R.C. (2000). *Motivation: Theories and principles* (4th ed.). Upper Saddle River, NJ: Prentice Hall.

Beckers, J., Dolmans, D., & Van Merriënboer, J. (2016). e-Portfolios enhancing students' self-directed learning: A systematic review of influencing factors. *Australasian Journal of Educational Technology, 32*(2), 32–46.

Bettinger, E., Ludvigsen, S., Rege, M., Solli, I. F., & Yeager, D. (2018). Increasing perseverance in math: Evidence from a field experiment in Norway. *Journal of Economic Behavior & Organization, 146*, 1–15.

Bingham, G. E., & Okagaki, L. (2012). Ethnicity and student engagement. In S. L. Christenson, A. L. Reschly, & C. Wylie (Eds.), *Handbook of research on student engagement* (pp. 65–95). New York, NY: Springer Science + Business Media.

Boaler, J. (2014). Research suggests that timed tests cause math anxiety. *Teaching Children Mathematics, 20*(8), 469–474.

Bong, M. (2001). Between- and within-domain relations of academic motivation among middle and high school students: Self-efficacy, task-value, and achievement goals. *Journal of Educational Psychology, 93*(1), 23–34.

Booker, K. C. (2006). School belonging and the African American adolescent: What do we know and where should we go? *High School Journal, 89*(4), 1–7.

Brophy, J. (2004). *Motivating students to learn.* New York, NY: Routledge.

Brophy, J. (2010). *Motivating students to learn* (3rd ed.). New York, NY: Routledge.

Brophy, J. E., & Everston, C. M. (1976). *Learning from teaching: A developmental perspective.* Boston, MA: Allyn & Bacon.

Brothen, T. (2012). Time limits on tests: Updating the 1-minute rule. *Teaching of Psychology, 39*(4), 288–292.

Carver-Thomas, D., & Darling-Hammond, L. (2019). The trouble with teacher turnover: How teacher attrition affects students and schools. *Education Policy Analysis Archives, 27*(36).

Cepeda, N. J., Vul, E., Rohrer, D., Wixted, J. T., & Pashler, H. (2008). Spacing effects in learning: A temporal ridgeline of optimal retention. *Psychological Science, 19*(11), 1095–1102.

Chen, X., Chung, J., & Hsiao, C. (2009). Peer interactions and relationships from a cross-cultural perspective. In K. H. Ruiin, W. M. Bukowski, & B. Laursen (Eds.), *Handbook of peer interactions, relationships, and groups* (pp. 432–451). New York, NY: Guilford.

Christenson, S. L., Reschly, A. L., & Wylie, C. (2012). *Handbook of research on student engagement.* New York, NY: Springer.

Cizek, G.J. (1999). *Cheating on tests: How to do it, detect it, and prevent it.* Mahwah, NJ: Lawrence Erlbaum.

Collier, L. (2015). Grabbing students. *Monitor on Psychology, 46*(6), 58.

Connell, J. P. (1990). Context, self, and action: A motivational analysis of self-system processes across the life span. In D. Cicchetti & M. Beeghly (Eds.), *The self in transition: Infancy to childhood.* (pp. 61–97). Chicago, IL: University of Chicago Press.

Connell, J. P., & Wellborn, J. G. (1991). Competence, autonomy, and relatedness: A motivational analysis of self-system processes. In M. R. Gunnar & L. A. Sroufe (Eds.), *Self processes and development.* (pp. 43–77). Hillsdale, NJ: Lawrence Erlbaum.

Conoley, C. W., & Conoley, J. C. (2009). Positive psychology for educators. In R. Gilman, E. S. Huebner, & M. J. Furlong (Eds.), *Handbook of positive psychology in schools.* (pp. 463–476). New York, NY: Routledge/Taylor & Francis Group.

Cornelius-White, J. (2007). Learner-centered teacher-student relationships are effective: A meta-analysis. *Review of Educational Research, 77*(1), 113–143.

D'Agostino, J. V., Rodgers, E. M., & Karpinski, A. C. (2010). The role of formative assessment in student achievement. In J. Hattie & E. M. Anderman (Eds.), *Visible learning guide to student achievement* (pp. 126–131). London, England: Routledge.

Davis, H. A. (2003). Conceptualizing the role and influence of student-teacher relationships on children's social and cognitive development. *Educational Psychologist, 38*(4), 207–234.

Davis, H. A. (2006). Exploring the contexts of relationship quality between middle school students and teachers. *Elementary School Journal, 106*(3), 193–223.

De Bruyckere, P., Kirschner, P. A., & Hulshof, C. D. (2015). *Urban myths about learning and education.* London, England: Elsevier.

Deci, E.L. (1992). The relation of interest to the motivation of behavior: A self-determination theory perspective. In K. A. Renninger, S. Hidi, & A. Krapp (Eds.), *The role of interest in learning and development* (pp. 43–70). Hillsdale, NJ: Lawrence Erlbaum.

Deci, E. L., Koestner, R., & Ryan, R. M. (2001). Extrinsic rewards and intrinsic motivation in education: Reconsidered once again. *Review of Educational Research, 71,* 1–27.

Deci, E. L., & Ryan, R. M. (1994). Promoting self-determined education. *Scandinavian Journal of Educational Research, 38,* 3–14.

Deci, E. L., & Ryan, R. M. (2012). Motivation, personality, and development within embedded social contexts: An overview of self-determination theory. In R. M. Ryan (Ed.), *The Oxford handbook of human motivation* (pp. 85–107). New York, NY: Oxford University Press.

Diamond, K. E., Justice, L. M., Siegler, R. S., Snyder, P. A., & National Center for Special Education Research (ED). (2013). *Synthesis of IES research on early intervention and early childhood education.* (NCSER 2013–3001). Washington, DC: National Center for Special Education Research. Institute of Education Sciences, U.S. Department of Education.

DiMenichi, B. C., & Tricomi, E. (2015). The power of competition: Effects of social motivation on attention, sustained physical effort, and learning. *Frontiers in Psychology, 6.* https://doi-org.proxy.lib.ohio-state.edu/10.3389/fpsyg.2015.01282

Durik, A. M., Vida, M., & Eccles, J. S. (2006). Task values and ability beliefs as predictors of high school literacy choices: A developmental analysis. *Journal of Educational Psychology, 98*(2), 382–393.

Dweck, C. S. (2006). *Mindset: The new psychology of success.* New York, NY: Ballantine Books.

Dweck, C. S., & Yeager, D. S. (2019). Mindsets: A view from two eras. *Perspectives on Psychological Science, 14*(3), 481–496.

Eccles, J. S., Midgley, C., Wigfield, A., Buchanan, C. M., Reuman, D., Flanagan, C., & Mac Iver, D. (1993). Development during adolescence: The impact of stage–environment fit on young adolescents' experiences in schools and in families. *American Psychologist, 48*(2), 90–101.

Eccles, J. S., & Roeser, R. W. (2011). School and community influences on human development. In M. H. Bornstein & M. E. Lamb (Eds.), *Developmental science: An advanced textbook* (6th ed., pp. 571–643). New York, NY: Psychology Press.

Eccles, J. S. , & Wang, M. T. (2012). Part I Commentary: So what is student engagement anyway? In S. L. Christenson, A. L. Reschly, & C. Wylie (Eds.), *Handbook of research on student engagement* (pp. 133–145). New York: Springer.

Eccles, J. S., & Wigfield, A. (2002). Motivational beliefs, values, and goals. *Annual Review of Psychology, 53*(1), 109.

Ewe, L. P. (2019). ADHD symptoms and the teacher–student relationship: A systematic literature review. *Emotional & Behavioural Difficulties, 24*(2), 136–155.

Fisher, M.R. (2019). Student assessment in teaching and learning. Vanderbilt University Center for Teaching and Learning. Downloaded November 25, 2019, from: https://cft.vanderbilt.edu/student-assessment-in-teaching-and-learning/

Fredricks, J. A., Blumenfeld, P. C., & Paris, A. H. (2004). School engagement: Potential of the concept, state of the evidence. *Review of Educational Research, 74*(1), 59–109.

Frenzel, A. C., Taxer, J. L., Schwab, C., & Kuhbandner, C. (2019). Independent and joint effects of teacher enthusiasm and motivation on student motivation and experiences: A field experiment. *Motivation & Emotion, 43*(2), 255–265.

Froiland, J. M., Worrell, F. C., & Oh, H. (2019). Teacher-student relationships, psychological need satisfaction, and happiness among diverse students. *Psychology in the Schools, 56*(5), 856–870.

Garcia, S. M., & Tor, A. (2009). The N-Effect: More competitors, less competition. *Psychological Science* (0956–7976), 20(7), 871–877. https://doi-org.proxy.lib.ohio-state.edu/10.1111/j.1467-9280.2009.02385.x

Garner, C. L., & Raudenbush, S. W. (1991). Neighborhood effects on educational attainment: A multilevel analysis. *Sociology of Education, 64*(4), 251–262.

Goetz, T., Preckel, F., Pekrun, R., & Hall, N. C. (2007). Emotional experiences during test taking: Does cognitive ability make a difference? *Learning & Individual Differences, 17*(1), 3–16.

Goodenow, C., & Grady, K.E. (1993). The relationship of school belonging and friends' values to academic motivation among urban adolescents. *Journal of Experimental Education, 62,* 60–71

Graham, S., & Taylor, A. Z. (2002). Ethnicity, gender, and the development of achievement values. In A. Wigfield & J. S. Eccles (Eds.), *Development of achievement motivation.* (pp. 121–146). San Diego, CA: Academic Press.

Granic, I., Lobel, A., & Engels, R. C. M. E. (2014). The benefits of playing video games. *American Psychologist, 69*(1), 66–78.

Gray, D. L., Hope, E. C., & Matthews, J. S. (2018). Black and belonging at school: A case for interpersonal, instructional, and institutional opportunity structures. *Educational Psychologist, 53*(2), 97–113.

Gray, M. R., & Steinberg, L. (1999). Unpacking authoritative parenting: Reassessing a multidimensional construct. *Journal of Marriage & Family, 61*(3), 574–587.

Grolnick, W.S., Lerner, R.E., Raftery-Helmer, J.N., & Allen, E.S. (2020). Parent involvement in learning. In J. Hattie & E.M. Anderman (Eds.), *Visible learning guide to student achievement* (pp. 66–72). New York, NY: Routledge.

Guskey, T. (2003). How classroom assessments improve learning. *Educational Leadership, 60*(5), 6–11.

Häfner, I., Flunger, B., Dicke, A., Gaspard, H., Brisson, B. M., Nagengast, B., & Trautwein, U. (2018). The role of family characteristics for students' academic outcomes: A person-centered approach. *Child Development, 89*(4), 1405–1422.

Harackiewicz, J. M., Rozek, C. S., Hulleman, C. S., & Hyde, J. S. (2012). Helping parents to motivate adolescents in mathematics and science: An experimental test of a utility-value intervention. *Psychological Science, 23*(8), 899–906.

Henderlong, J., & Lepper, M. R. (2002). The effects of praise on children's intrinsic motivation: A review and synthesis. *Psychological Bulletin, 128*(5), 774–795.

Hidi, S. (2001). Interest, reading, and learning: Theoretical and practical considerations. *Educational Psychology Review, 13*(3), 191–209.

Hidi, S., Weiss, J., Berndorff, D., & Nolan, J. (1998). The role of gender, instruction and a cooperative learning technique in science education across formal and informal settings. In L. Hoffmann, A. Krapp, K. A. Renninger, & J. Baumert (Eds.), *Interest and learning: Proceedings of the Seeon conference on interest and gender* (pp. 215–227). Kiel, Germany: IPN.

Higgins, K., Huscroft-D'Angelo, J., & Crawford, L. (2019). Effects of technology in mathematics on achievement, motivation, and attitude: A meta-analysis. *Journal of Educational Computing Research, 57*(2), 283–319.

Huang, F. L., Lewis, C., Cohen, D. R., Prewett, S., & Herman, K. (2018). Bullying involvement, teacher-student relationships, and psychosocial outcomes. *School Psychology Quarterly, 33*(2), 223–234.

Hulleman, C. S., Kosovich, J. J., Barron, K. E., & Daniel, D. B. (2017). Making connections: Replicating and extending the utility value intervention in the classroom. *Journal of Educational Psychology, 109*(3), 387–404.

Hunsley, J., Lee, C. M., & Wood, J. M. (2003). Controversial and questionable assessment techniques. In S. O. Lilienfeld, S. J. Lynn, & J. M. Lohr (Eds.), *Science and pseudoscience in clinical psychology.* (pp. 39–76). New York, NY: Guilford Press.

Jodl, K. M., Michael, A., Malanchuk, O., Eccles, J. S., & Sameroff, A. (2001). Parents' roles in shaping early adolescents' occupational aspirations. *Child Development, 72*(4), 1247–1265.

Johnson, D.W., & Johnson, R.T. (1998). *Learning together and alone: Cooperative, competitive, and individualistic learning* (5th ed.). Boston, MA: Allyn & Bacon.

Julien, M., Stratton, M., & Clayton, R. (2018). History is "not" boring: Using social media to bring labor history alive. *Management Teaching Review, 3*(3), 208–220.

Kain, E. (2011). President Obama says standardized tests make education boring. *Forbes*, March 29, 2011. Retrieved from https://www.forbes.com/sites/erikkain/

2011/03/29/president-obama-says-standardized-tests-make-education-boring-dont-adequately-measure-performance/#35f263e555db

Kim, S. W., & Hill, N. E. (2015). Including fathers in the picture: A meta-analysis of parental involvement and students' academic achievement. *Journal of Educational Psychology, 107*(4), 919–934.

Kluger, A.N., & DeNisi, A. (1996). The effect of feedback interventions on performance: A historical review, meta-analysis, and a preliminary feedback intervention theory. *Psychological Bulletin, 119*, 254–284.

Koca, F. (2016). Motivation to learn and teacher-student relationship. *Journal of International Education and Leadership, 6*(2). Retrieved from http://search.ebscohost.com.proxy.lib.ohio-state.edu/login.aspx? direct=true&db=eric&AN=EJ1135209&site=ehost-live

Koenka, A. C., & Anderman, E. M. (2019) Personalized feedback as a strategy for improving motivation and performance among middle school students, *Middle School Journal, 50*(5), 15–22. DOI: 10.1080/00940771.2019.1674768

Kohn, A. (1986). *The case against competition.* Boston, MA: Houghton Mifflin Company.

LaRose, R, Kim, J., & Peng, W. (2010). Social networking: Addictive, compulsive, problematic, or just another media habit. In Z. Papacharissi (Ed.), *A networked self: Identity, community, and culture on social network sites* (pp. 59–81). New York, NY: Routledge.

Lauermann, F., Tsai, Y.-M., & Eccles, J. S. (2017). Math-related career aspirations and choices within Eccles et al.'s expectancy–value theory of achievement-related behaviors. *Developmental Psychology, 53*(8), 1540–1559.

Laursen, B., & Collins, W. A. (2009). Parent-child relationships during adolescence. In R. M. Lerner & L. Steinberg (Eds.), *Handbook of adolescent psychology: Contextual influences on adolescent development.,* (3rd ed., Vol. 2, pp. 3–42). Hoboken, NJ: John Wiley & Sons Inc.

Lemon, N., & Garvis, S. (2016). Pre-service teacher self-efficacy in digital technology. *Teachers and Teaching: Theory and Practice, 22*(3), 387–408.

Lepper, M. R. (1988). Motivational considerations in the study of instruction. *Cognition & Instruction, 5*(4), 289.

Lepper, M. R., Greene, D., & Nisbett, R. E. (1973). Understanding children's intrinsic interest with extrinsic rewards. *Journal of Personality and Social Psychology, 28*, 129–137.

Lepper, M. R., & Hodell, M. (1989). Intrinsic motivation in the classroom. In C. Ames & R. Ames (eds.), *Research on motivation in education, Vol. 3: Goals and cognitions* (pp. 73–105). San Diego, CA: Academic Press.

Leyendecker, B., Harwood, R. L., Comparini, L., & Yalçinkaya, A. (2005). Socioeconomic status, ethnicity, and parenting. In T. Luster & L. Okagaki (Eds.), *Parenting: An ecological perspective,* (2nd ed., pp. 319–341). Mahwah, NJ: Lawrence Erlbaum.

Lleras, C., & Rangel, C. (2009). Ability grouping practices in elementary school and African American/Hispanic achievement. *American Journal of Education, 115*(2), 279–304.

Lorain, P. (2019). *Teaching that emphasizes active engagement.* National Education Association, Washington, DC. Retrieved from http://www.nea.org/tools/16708.htm

Maehr, M. L. (1976). Continuing motivation: An analysis of a seldom considered educational outcome. *Review of Educational Outcome, 46* (3), 443–462.

Maehr, M. L., & Midgley, C. (1991). Enhancing student motivation: A schoolwide approach. *Educational Psychologist, 26*(3/4), 399–427.

Mandinach, E. B. , & Lash, A. A. (2016). Assessment illuminating pathways to learning. In L. Como & E. M. Anderman (Eds.), *Handbook of educational psychology,* 3rd Ed. (pp. 390–401). New York: Routledge/Taylor & Francis Group.

Marks, H. M. (2000). Student engagement in instructional activity: Patterns in the elementary, middle, and high school years. *American Educational Research Journal, 37*(1), 153–184.

Maslow, A. (1954). *Motivation and personality.* New York, NY: Harper.

May, C. (2018, May 29). The problem with "Learning Styles." *Scientific American.* Retrieved from: https://www.scientificamerican.com/article/the-problem-with-learning-styles/

McCaslin, M., & Good, T.L. (1992). Compliant cognition: The misalliance of management and instructional goals in current school reform. *Educational Researcher, 21*(3), 4–17.

McLoyd, V. C., Kaplan, R., Purtell, K. M., Bagley, E., Hardaway, C. R., & Smalls, C. (2009). Poverty and socioeconomic disadvantage in adolescence. In R. M. Lerner & L. Steinberg (Eds.), *Handbook of adolescent psychology: Contextual influences on adolescent development* (3rd ed., vol. 2, pp. 444–491). Hoboken, NJ: John Wiley & Sons Inc.

Midgley, C., & Feldlaufer, H. (1987). Students' and teachers' decision-making fit before and after the transition to junior high school. *The Journal of Early Adolescence, 7*(2), 225–241.

Milo, G. (2015). Why do students hate history? *Education Week* (September 23). Downloaded from: https://www.edweek.org/ew/articles/2015/09/23/why-do-students-hate-history.html

Mitchell, M. (1993). Situational interest: Its multifaceted structure in the secondary school mathematics classroom. *Journal of Educational Psychology, 85*, 424–436.

Murayama, K., & Elliot, A. J. (2012). The competition–performance relation: A meta-analytic review and test of the opposing processes model of competition and performance. *Psychological Bulletin, 138*(6), 1035–1070.

Murdock, T. B., & Anderman, E. M. (2006). Motivational perspectives on student cheating: Toward an integrated model of academic dishonesty. *Educational Psychologist, 41*, 129–145.

Murray, C., & Pianta, R. (2007). The importance of teacher-student relationships for adolescents with high incidence disabilities. *Theory Into Practice, 46*(2), 105–112.

Musu-Gillette, L. E., Wigfield, A., Harring, J. R., & Eccles, J. S. (2015). Trajectories of change in students' self-concepts of ability and values in math and college major choice. *Educational Research and Evaluation, 21*(4), 343–370.

Nagy, G., Trautwein, U., Baumert, J., Koller, O., & Garrett, J. (2006). Gender and course selection in upper secondary education: Effects of academic self-concept and intrinsic value. *Educational Research and Evaluation, 12*(4), 323–345.

Nancekivell, S. E., Shah, P., & Gelman, S. A. (2019). Maybe they're born with it, or maybe it's experience: Toward a deeper understanding of the learning style myth. *Journal of Educational Psychology.* Advance online publication. http://dx.doi.org/10.1037/edu00003

National Center for Education Statistics. (2008). *Schools and staffing survey.* Retrieved from: https://nces.ed.gov/surveys/sass/tables/sass0708_035_s1s.asp

National Science Foundation. (2019). *Science and engineering labor force.* Washington, DC: NSF. Retrieved from: https://ncses.nsf.gov/pubs/nsb20198

New York Times (1992, 21 October). *Mattel says it erred; teen talk Barbie turns silent on math.* Retrieved from https://www.nytimes.com/1992/10/21/business/company-news-mattel-says-it-erred-teen-talk-barbie-turns-silent-on-math.html

Newmann, F. (1991). Student engagement in academic work: Expanding the perspective on secondary school effectiveness. In J. R. Bliss & W. A. Firestone (Eds.), *Rethinkng effective schools: Research and practice* (pp. 58–76). Englewood Cliffs, NJ: Prentice Hall.

Nicholls, J. G. (1990). What is ability and why are we mindful of it? A developmental perspective. In R. J. Sternberg & J. Kolligian Jr. (Eds.), *Competence considered* (pp. 11–40). New Haven, CT: Yale University Press.

Nichols, S. L., & Berliner, D. C. (2008). Testing the joy out of learning. *Educational Leadership, 65*(6), 14–18.

Noddings, N. (2012). The caring relation in teaching. *Oxford Review of Education, 38*(6), 771–781.

Oakes, J. (1990). *Multiplying inequalities: The effects of race, social class, and tracking on opportunities to learn in mathematics and science.* Santa Monica, CA: Rand.

Oakes, J., Gamoran, A., & Page, R. (1992). Curriculum differentiation: Opportunities, outcomes, and meanings. In P. Jackson (Ed.), *Handbook of research on curriculum* (pp. 570–608). New York, NY: Macmillan.

Olson, L. (2001). Overboard on testing? *Education Week* (January 11). Retrieved from https://www.edweek.org/ew/articles/2001/01/11/overboard-on-testing.html

Paris, S. G., Roth, J. L., & Turner, J. C. (2000). Developing disillusionment: Students' perceptions of academic achievement tests. *Issues in Education, 6*(1/2), 17.

Parker, L. E., & Lepper, M. R. (1987). *The effects of fantasy context on children's learning and motivation.* Retrieved from http://search.ebscohost.com.proxy.lib.ohio-state.edu/login.aspx?direct=true&db=eric&AN=ED294676&site=ehost-live

Pas, E. T., Cash, A. H., O'Brennan, L., Debnam, K. J., & Bradshaw, C. P. (2015). Profiles of classroom behavior in high schools: Associations with teacher behavior management strategies and classroom composition. *Journal of School Psychology, 53*(2), 137–148.

Pat El, R., Tillema, H., & van Koppen, S. W. M. (2012). Effects of formative feedback on intrinsic motivation: Examining ethnic differences. *Learning & Individual Differences, 22*(4), 449–454.

Patall, E.A., & Zambrano, J. (2019). Facilitating student outcomes by supporting autonomy: Implications for practice and policy. *Policy Insights from the Behavioral and Brain Sciences, 6*(2), 115–122.

Pianta, R., Downer, J., & Hamre, B. (2016). Quality in early education classrooms: Definitions, gaps, and systems. *Future of Children, 26*(2), 119–137.

Pink, D.H. (2009). *Drive: The surprising truth about what motivates us.* New York, NY: Riverhead Books.

Quin, D. (2017). Longitudinal and contextual associations between teacher-student relationships and student engagement: A systematic review. *Review of Educational Research, 87*(2), 345–387.

Raphael, L. M., Pressley, M., & Mohan, L. (2008). Engaging instruction in middle school classrooms: An observational study of nine teachers. *Elementary School Journal, 109*(1), 61–81.

Redding, C. (2019). A teacher like me: A review of the effect of student-teacher racial/ethnic matching on teacher perceptions of students and student academic and behavioral outcomes. *Review of Educational Research, 89*(4), 499–535

Reeve, J. (2006). Extrinsic rewards and inner motivation. In C. M. Evertson & C. S. Weinstein (Eds.), *Handbook of classroom management: Research, practice, and contemporary issues* (pp. 645–664). Mahwah, NJ: Lawrence Erlbaum.

Reeve, J., & Tseng, C.-M. (2011). Agency as a fourth aspect of students' engagement during learning activities. *Contemporary Educational Psychology.* doi:10.1016/j.cedpsych.2011.05.002

Renninger K. A., & Hidi, S. (2011). Revisiting the conceptualization, measurement, and generation of interest. *Educational Psychologist, 46*(3), 168–184.

Rideout, V., & Robb, M. B. (2018). *Social media, social life: Teens reveal their experiences.* San Francisco, CA: Common Sense Media.

Rogowsky, B. A., Calhoun, B. M., & Tallal, P. (2015). Matching learning style to instructional method: Effects on comprehension. *Journal of Educational Psychology, 107*, 64–78. http://dx.doi.org/10.1037/ a0037478

Rohrer, D., & Pashler, H. (2010). Recent research on human learning challenges conventional instructional strategies. *Educational Researcher, 39*(5), 406–412.

Roorda, D. L., Jak, S., Zee, M., Oort, F. J., & Koomen, H. M. Y. (2017). Affective teacher-student relationships and students' engagement and achievement: A meta-analytic update and test of the mediating role of engagement. *School Psychology Review, 46*(3), 239–261.

Roseth, C. J., Johnson, D. W., & Johnson, R. T. (2008). Promoting early adolescents' achievement and peer relationships: The effects of cooperative, competitive, and individualistic goal structures. *Psychological Bulletin, 134*(2), 223–246.

Ross, L. (2018). From the fundamental attribution error to the truly fundamental attribution error and beyond: My research journey. *Perspectives on Psychological Science, 13*(6), 750–769.

Roth, J. L., Paris, S. G., & Turner, J. C. (2000). Students' perceived utility and reported use of test-taking strategies. *Issues in Education, 6*(1/2), 67.

Rumberger, R. W., & Rotermund, S. (2012). The relationship between engagement and high school dropout. In S. L. Christenson, A. L. Reschly & C. Wylie (Eds.), *Handbook of research on student engagement.* (pp. 491–513). New York, NY: Springer Science + Business Media.

Ryan, R. M., & Deci, E. L. (2017). *Self-determination theory: Basic psychological needs in motivation, development, and wellness.* New York, NY: Guilford Press.

Ryan, R. M., & Weinstein, N. (2009). Undermining quality teaching and learning: A self-determination theory perspective on high-stakes testing. *Theory and Research in Education, 7*(2), 224–233.

Sarrasin, J. B., Nenciovici, L., Foisy, L.-M. B., Allaire-Duquette, G., Riopel, M., & Masson, S. (2018). Effects of teaching the concept of neuroplasticity to induce a growth mindset on motivation, achievement, and brain activity: A meta-analysis. *Trends in Neuroscience and Education, 12,* 22–31.

Schraw, G., Flowerday, T., & Lehman, S. (2001). Increasing situational interest in the classroom. *Educational Psychology Review, 13*(3), 211–224.

Schraw, G., & Lehman, S. (2001). Situational interest: A review of the literature and directions for future research. *Educational Psychology Review, 13*(1), 23–52.

Schug, M. C., Todd, R. J., & Beery, R. (1982, November). *Why kids don't like social studies.* Paper presented at the annual meeting of the National Council for Social Studies. Boston, MA.

Schunk, D. H. (1984). Enhancing self-efficacy and achievement through rewards and goals: Motivational and informational effects. *Journal of Educational Research, 78*(1), 29–34.

Schunk, D.H., Meece, J. L., & Pintrich, P. R. (2014). *Motivation in education: Theory, research, and applications.* Boston, MA: Pearson.

Shavelson, R. J., Yue Yin, Furtak, E. M., Araceli Ruiz-Primo, M., Ayala, C. C., Young, D. B., Tomita, M. K., Brando, P. R., & Pottenger III, F. M. (2008). On the role and impact of formative assessment on science inquiry teaching and learning. In *Assessing Science Learning: Perspectives from Research & Practice* (pp. 21–36). Arlington, VA: National Science Teachers Association.

Simpkins, S. D., Fredricks J. A., & Eccles, J. S. (2012). Charting the Eccles' expectancy-value model from mothers' beliefs in childhood to youths' activities in adolescence. *Developmental Psychology, 48*(4), 1019–1032.

Simzar, R. M., Martinez, M., Rutherford, T., Domina, T., & Conley, A. M. (2015). Raising the stakes: How students' motivation for mathematics associates with high- and low-stakes test achievement. *Learning & Individual Differences*, *39*, 49–63.

Slaten, C. D., Ferguson, J. K., Allen, K.-A., Brodrick, D.-V., & Waters, L. (2016). School belonging: A review of the history, current trends, and future directions. *Educational and Developmental Psychologist*, *33*, 1–15.

Slavin, R. E., & National Education Association, W. D. (1991). *Student team learning: A practical guide to cooperative learning.* (3rd ed.). Retrieved from http://search.ebscohost.com/login.aspx?direct=true&db=eric&AN=ED339518&site=ehost-live

Sparks, S. D. (2019). U.S. students and teachers top global peers for time spent in school in OECD study. *Education Week* (September 10). Retrieved from http://blogs.edweek.org/edweek/inside-school-research/2019/09/OECD_education_at_a_glance_2019.html

Spilt, J. L., & Hughes, J. N. (2015). African American children at risk of increasingly conflicted teacher-student relationships in elementary school. *School Psychology Review*, *44*(3), 306–314.

Steenbergen-Hu, S., Makel, M. C., & Olszewski-Kubilius, P. (2016). What one hundred years of research says about the effects of ability grouping and acceleration on K–12 students' academic achievement: Findings of two second-order meta-analyses. *Review of Educational Research*, *86*(4), 849–899.

Stipek, D. (2011). Classroom practices and children's motivation to learn. In E. Zigler, W. S. Gilliam, & W. S. Barnett (Eds.), *The pre-K debates: Current controversies and issues.* (pp. 98–103). Baltimore, MD: Paul H Brookes Publishing.

Tereshchenko, B. F., Archer, L., Jeremy Hodgen, Mazenod, A., Taylor, B., Pepper D., & Travers, M. (2019) Learners' attitudes to mixed-attainment grouping: Examining the views of students of high, middle, and low attainment. *Research Papers in Education*, *34*(4), 425–444. doi: 10.1080/02671522.2018.1452962

Tole, S. (2017). How societal norms work against women choosing STEM careers. *Economic Times* (September 26). Retrieved from https://economictimes.indiatimes.com/small-biz/entrepreneurship/how-societal-norms-work-against-women-choosing-stem-careers/articleshow/60804962.cms?from=mdr

Triplett, C. F., & Barksdale, M. A. (2005). Third through sixth graders' perceptions of high-stakes testing. *Journal of Literacy Research*, *37*(2), 237–260.

Tze, V., Daniels, L., & Klassen, R. (2016). Evaluating the relationship between boredom and academic outcomes: A meta-analysis. *Educational Psychology Review, 28*(1), 119–144.

Vasquez, A., Patall, E., Fong, C., Corrigan, A., & Pine, L. (2016). Parent autonomy support, academic achievement, and psychosocial functioning: A meta-analysis of research. *Educational Psychology Review, 28*(3), 605–644.

Walker, T. (2014). NEA Survey: Nearly half of teachers consider leaving profession due to standardized testing. *NEA Today* (Nov. 2). Retrieved from: http://neatoday.org/2014/11/02/nea-survey-nearly-half-of-teachers-consider-leaving-profession-due-to-standardized-testing-2/

Wang, M. T., Chow, A., Degol, J. L., & Eccles, J. S. (2017). Does everyone's motivational beliefs about physical science decline in secondary school?: Heterogeneity of adolescents' achievement motivation trajectories in physics and chemistry. *Journal of Youth and Adolescence, 46*(8), 1821–1838.

Wang, M. T., & Eccles, J. S. (2012). Adolescent behavioral, emotional, and cognitive engagement trajectories in school and their differential relations to educational success. *Journal of Research on Adolescence, 22*(1), 31–39.

Wang, M. T., Eccles, J. S., & Kenny, S. (2013). Not lack of ability but more choice: Individual and gender differences in choice of careers in science, technology, engineering, and mathematics. *Psychological Science* (0956–7976), *24*(5), 770–775.

Watt, H. M. G., Shapka, J. D., Morris, Z. A., Durik, A. M., Keating, D. P., & Eccles, J. S. (2012). Gendered motivational processes affecting high school mathematics participation, educational aspirations, and career plans: A comparison of samples from Australia, Canada, and the United States. *Developmental Psychology, 48*(6), 1594–1611.

Weinstein, R. S., Marshall, H., Brattenasi, K., & Middlestadt, S. (1982). Student perceptions of differential treatment in open and traditional classrooms. *Journal of Educational Psychology, 74*, 678–692.

Wentzel, K. R. (1997). (1997). Student motivation in middle school: The role of perceived pedagogical caring. *Journal of Educational Psychology, 89*, 411–419.

Whitaker, D., Graham, C., Severtson, S., Debra Furr-Holden, C., & Latimer, W. (2012). Neighborhood & family effects on learning motivation among urban African American middle school youth. *Journal of Child & Family Studies, 21*(1), 131–138.

Wigfield, A., & Eccles, J. S. (1992). The development of achievement values: A theoretical analysis. *Developmental Review, 12*, 265–310.

Wigfield, A., & Eccles, J. S. (2002). The development of competence beliefs, expectancies for success, and achievement values from childhood through adolescence. In A. Wigfield & J. S. Eccles (Eds.), *Development of achievement motivation.* (pp. 91–120). San Diego, CA: Academic Press.

Wigfield, A., Eccles, J. S., Fredricks, J. A., Simpkins, S., Roeser, R. W., & Schiefele, U. (2015). Development of achievement motivation and engagement. In M. E. Lamb & R. M. Lerner (Eds.), *Handbook of child psychology and developmental science: Socioemotional processes.* (7th ed., vol. 3, pp. 657–700). Hoboken, NJ: John Wiley & Sons Inc.

Williams, L. M., Hedrick, W. B., & Tuschinski, L. (2008). Motivation: Going beyond testing to a lifetime of reading. *Childhood Education, 84*(3), 135.

Wong, C. A., & Paris, S. G. (2000). Students' beliefs about classroom tests and standardized tests. *Issues in Education, 6*(1/2), 47.

Xie, K., & Ke, F. (2011). The role of students' motivation in peer-moderated asynchronous online discussions. *British Journal of Educational Technology, 42*(6), 916–930.

Yeager, D. S., Dahl, R. E., & Dweck, C. S. (2018). Why interventions to influence adolescent behavior often fail but could succeed. *Perspectives on Psychological Science, 13*, 101–122.

Zimmer-Gembeck, M. J., Chipeur, H. M., & Hanisch, M. (2006). Relationships at school and stage-environment fit as resources for adolescent engagement and achievement. *Journal of Adolescence, 29*(6), 911–933.

INDEX

Confident Teachers, Inspired Learners

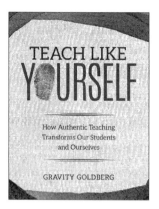

GRAVITY GOLDBERG

In *Teach Like Yourself*, Gravity Goldberg applies ideas from fields of psychology, education, and science to name five key habits involving core beliefs, practice, relationships, professional growth, and one's whole self.

SERENA PARISER

This handy guide offers 50 proven best practices for managing today's classroom, complete with just-in-time tools and relatable teacher-to-teacher anecdotes and advice.

VICTORIA LENTFER

Whether you're new to teaching, working with at-risk students, or simply looking for new strategies, the CALM method provides an actionable framework for redirecting student behavior.

LISA WESTMAN

Full of step-by-step guidance, this book shows you how to build collaborative student teacher relationships and incorporate student voice and choice in the process of planning for student-driven differentiation.

To order your copies, visit corwin.com

No matter where you are in your professional journey, Corwin aims to ease the many demands teachers face on a daily basis with accessible strategies that benefit ALL learners. Through research-based, high-quality content, we offer practical guidance on a wide range of topics, including curriculum planning, learning frameworks, classroom design and management, and much more. Our books, videos, consulting, and online resources are developed by renowned educators and designed for easy implementation that will provide tangible results for you and your students.

WARREN BERGER, ELISE FOSTER

Written to be both inspirational and practical, *Beautiful Questions in the Classroom* shows educators how they can transform their classrooms into cultures of curiosity.

SERENA PARISER, EDWARD F. DEROCHE

Gain time in each day, reduce stress, and improve your classroom learning environment with 35 practical, teacher-proven strategies for managing time and setting personal boundaries.

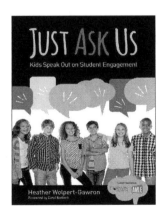

HEATHER WOLPERT-GAWRON

Based on over 1000 nationwide student surveys, these 10 deep engagement strategies help you implement achievement-based cooperative learning. Includes video and a survey sample.

CATLIN R. TUCKER

Balance With Blended Learning provides teachers with practical strategies to actively engage students in setting goals, monitoring development, reflecting on growth, using feedback, assessing work quality, and communicating their progress with parents.

CORWIN

A SAGE Publishing Company

Helping educators make the greatest impact

CORWIN HAS ONE MISSION: to enhance education through intentional professional learning.

We build long-term relationships with our authors, educators, clients, and associations who partner with us to develop and continuously improve the best evidence-based practices that establish and support lifelong learning.

Made in the USA
Las Vegas, NV
07 October 2021